G000146454

POCKET M

Management

Level 4

MCI, Russell Square House, 10-12 Russell Square, London WC1B 5BZ
Telephone 0171 872 9000
Website http://www.bbi.co.uk/mci
e-mail nfmed_mci@compuserve.com
Registered Charity No. 1002554

Management Charter Initiative is the operating arm of the National
Forum for Management Education and Development.

The National Occupational Standard for Management was developed by MCI with funding from
the Department for Education and Employment.

This material is Crown Copyright © and is reproduced under licence from the Controller of
Her Majesty's Stationery Office. All rights reserved. No part of this publication may be
reproduced, stored in a retrieval system, or transmitted in any form or by any means,
electronic, mechanical, photocopying, recording or otherwise, without the prior permission in
writing of the Publishers. Copies of the Management Standards contained within this
publication may be made for educational purposes only, provided no commercial benefit is
intended or derived. Crown Copyright © must always be acknowledged.

First published 1998

ISBN 1 897587 76 7

Text processing and typesetting by Digital Type
Printed and bound in Great Britain by Cambridge University Press

Contents

Acknowledgements

MCI gratefully acknowledges the assistance of over 4,000 managers and hundreds of employing organisations from all sectors of the economy who participated in the revision and piloting of these standards; the financial support of the Department for Education and Employment; and the Steering Group members, individuals, consultants and MCI staff who have contributed to the development and authorship of this publication.

Management Standards and Qualifications

Developed through consultation with tens of thousands of managers throughout the private, public and voluntary sectors, the Management Standards define benchmarks of best practice in management in the UK today. They describe the standard of performance which is expected of you in the wide variety of functions you carry out as a manager.

If you can prove to an assessor that you consistently perform to these *National Standards*, you can be awarded a National Vocational Qualification (NVQ) or Scottish Vocational Qualification (SVQ). NVQs and SVQs in Management are available at the three highest levels, known as levels 3, 4 and 5 (levels 1 and 2 cover technical, administrative and other non-management functions).

This booklet *Management Level 4* covers all the units of the Management Standards at NVQ/SVQ level 4. It is for you if you are a practising manager with responsibility for:

- allocating work to others
- achieving specific results by using resources effectively
- carrying out policy in your defined area of authority
- controlling limited financial budgets, and
- contributing to broader activities such as change programmes and recruitment.

If you are aspiring to become a manager, you will find these standards a useful guide to what will be expected of you as a manager working at this level.

Units of Competence

The Management Standards are expressed in a number of *units of competence*, each unit describing a specific management function. The units contain *performance criteria*, clear statements which allow you to assess whether you are performing to the national standard. If you are taking an NVQ or SVQ, your assessor will need to be sure you consistently meet all these criteria in order to certify that you are competent.

The standards specify *knowledge requirements*, what you need to know and understand in order to perform to the national standard. They also identify the *personal competencies*, the skills and attitudes which are essential for effective performance, described as behaviours which it is possible to observe. You can therefore read appropriate management books or attend development programmes to ensure you have the necessary knowledge and skills. If you are unsure about your performance in a particular area, you can use the Management Standards to diagnose the knowledge or skills development you require.

Finally, the standards specify *evidence requirements*. These clearly state the evidence you need to convince your NVQ/SVQ assessor or your line manager that you are competent.

Coverage of Management Level 4

Management Level 4 covers the full range of general management activities which managers working at this level are expected to carry out. It does not, however, cover specialist functions (such as sales, accounting or engineering) which are covered by other, specialist standards.

You will find your work as a manager is reflected in the four generic key roles: *A Manage Activities, B Manage Resources, C*

1

Management Standards and Qualifications

Manage People and *D Manage Information*. You may also have some specialist responsibilities which are covered in the specialist management key roles of *E Manage Energy*, *F Manage Quality* and *G Manage Projects*.

Unit A2 *Manage activities to meet requirements* is about managing activities and conditions in the workplace to meet the requirements of your organisation and your customers.

Unit A4 *Contribute to improvements at work* covers making significant contributions to improving team and organisational performance.

Unit B2 *Manage the use of physical resources* covers planning the use of the resources you and your team need, obtaining those resources, ensuring the availability of supplies, and monitoring the use of resources.

Unit B3 *Manage the use of financial resources* covers making recommendations for the use of financial resources and controlling expenditure against budgets.

Unit C2 *Develop your own resources* is about developing your knowledge and skills and managing your time and resources so that you can meet your objectives.

Unit C5 *Develop productive working relationships* is about developing relationships with colleagues within your organisation.

Unit C8 *Select personnel for activities* is about recruiting and selecting the people you need to carry out your work activities.

Unit C10 *Develop teams and individuals to enhance performance* covers identifying people's development needs, planning their development and using a variety of means to improve team performance.

Unit C13 *Manage the performance of teams and individuals* covers allocating work, agreeing objectives, setting out plans and methods of working, monitoring and evaluating work and providing feedback to people on their performance.

Unit C15 *Respond to poor performance in the team* is about helping to deal with team members whose performance is unsatisfactory, including contributing to disciplinary and grievance procedures.

Unit D2 *Facilitate meetings* covers leading meetings and contributing to meetings so that objectives can be achieved.

Unit D4 *Provide information to support decision making* covers obtaining, recording, storing and analysing information. It also covers advising and informing other people.

The 'E' units, 'F' units and 'G' units are specialist units and cover managing energy, quality and projects respectively.

Gaining a Management NVQ or SVQ

To be assessed for a Management NVQ or SVQ, you must register with an approved centre (details available from MCI). In contrast to academic qualifications, with NVQs and SVQs there is no prescribed course of study. The centre will provide you with advice on any areas where you need to develop new knowledge and skills. The centre itself may offer management development programmes, or it may refer you to other management courses, text books, open and flexible learning schemes or other development activities.

The centre will also provide you with guidance on how to prepare for assessment and allocate you an assessor who will assess your competence. If you are taking and NVQ/SVQ in Management Level 4, you will be assessed against the 5 mandatory units (highlighted in bold on the page opposite), at least one unit from key role B, plus any three other units which you are free to choose.

You will need to gather evidence of your competence which will include products and outcomes of your work activities as well as short reports of your own and statements from others who have observed your performance. You will submit this evidence to your assessor together with your claim for competence. After an assessment interview, your assessor will make one of three credit recommendations: that you are competent, not yet competent, or that you have not provided sufficient evidence to make a decision. If you are assessed as competent, you will be awarded your NVQ or SVQ.

Continuously improving your performance

Your use of the Management Standards does not end with your award of the NVQ or SVQ. When you are familiar with the standards and their performance criteria, it is easy to use them on a daily basis to check that you are working to the benchmarks of best practice. As you take on new tasks and responsibilities, you can prepare to meet these by developing the necessary knowledge and skills which you will find in other specialist standards. If you are given greater authority and autonomy as a manager, you may wish to start looking at

higher level Management Standards and preparing for an NVQ or SVQ in Management at level 5.

Management

Level 4

NVQ/SVQ

Mandatory units
Candidates take FIVE mandatory units
A2, A4, C2, C5, D4 *plus* either B2 or B3

Manage activities to meet requirements

Unit summary

This unit is about managing activities and conditions in the workplace to meet the requirements of your organisation and your customers. This involves agreeing the outputs required, planning work activities to deliver these outputs and monitoring these activities to make sure quality requirements have been met. It also involves maintaining a healthy, safe and productive work environment and continuously looking for ways to improve the processes involved.

This unit contains three elements

A2.1 *Implement plans to meet customer requirements*
A2.2 *Maintain a healthy, safe and productive work environment*
A2.3 *Ensure products and services meet quality requirements*.

Personal competencies

In performing effectively in this unit, you will show that you

Building teams
- keep others informed about plans and progress
- clearly identify what is required of others
- invite others to contribute to planning and organising work

Communicating
- identify the information needs of listeners
- adopt communication styles appropriate to listeners and situations, including selecting an appropriate time and place
- use a variety of media and communication aids to reinforce points and maintain interest

Focusing on results
- maintain a focus on objectives
- tackle problems and take advantage of opportunities as they arise
- actively seek to do things better
- use change as an opportunity for improvement
- monitor quality of work and progress against plans

Influencing others
- present yourself positively to others
- create and prepare strategies for influencing others
- use a variety of means to influence others

Thinking and taking decisions
- break processes down into tasks and activities
- identify a range of elements in and perspectives on a situation
- identify implications, consequences or causal relationships in a situation
- take decisions which are realistic for the situation.

Manage activities to meet requirements

Element A2.1

Implement plans to meet customer requirements

Performance criteria

You must ensure that

a) you agree **requirements** with **customers** in sufficient detail to allow work to be planned effectively

b) your plans allow **requirements** to be met within agreed time scales

c) you explain plans to **relevant people** in sufficient detail and at an appropriate level and pace

d) you confirm with **relevant people** their understanding of, and commitment to, your plans

e) you follow organisational procedures for recording your plans

f) you give opportunities to **relevant people** to make recommendations for improving plans.

Knowledge requirements

You need to know and understand

Communication
- how to communicate effectively with team members, colleagues, line managers and people outside your organisation

Customer relations
- the importance of a focus on customer requirements and quality issues, and your role and responsibilities in relation to this
- the differences between internal and external customers

Involvement and motivation
- how to encourage and enable team members, colleagues and line managers to help to improve efficiency

Organisational context
- the records which you need to complete and how this should be done

Planning
- how to identify customer requirements to a level of detail sufficient for planning work
- the principles of planning work activities, setting objectives and priorities to ensure requirements are met efficiently.

Evidence requirements

You must prove that you *implement plans to meet customer requirements* to the National Standard of competence.

To do this, you must provide evidence to convince your assessor that you consistently meet **all** the performance criteria.

Your evidence must be the result of real work activities undertaken by yourself. Evidence from simulated activities is **not** acceptable for this element.

You must show evidence that you agree **all** the following **requirements**
- quality
- quantity
- delivery
- health and safety.

You must show evidence that you agree requirements with **one** of the following types of **customer**
- internal
- external.

You must also show that you explain work activities and provide opportunities for making recommendations to **one** of the following types of **relevant people**
- team members
- colleagues working at your level
- higher-level managers or sponsors
- people outside your organisation.

You must, however, convince your assessor that you have the necessary knowledge, understanding and skills to be able to perform competently in respect of **all** types of **customers** and **relevant people**, listed above

Manage activities to meet requirements

Element A2.2

Maintain a healthy, safe and productive work environment

Performance criteria

You must ensure that

a) you inform **relevant people** about their legal and organisational responsibilities for maintaining a healthy, safe and productive **work environment**

b) you make sufficient support available to **relevant people** to ensure they can work in a healthy, safe and productive way

c) you provide opportunities for **relevant people** to make recommendations for improving the **work environment**

d) the **work environment** under your control conforms to organisational and legal requirements

e) the **work environment** under your control is as conducive to healthy, safe and productive working as possible within organisational constraints

f) you respond to breaches in health and safety requirements promptly and in line with organisational and legal requirements

g) you make recommendations for improving the **work environment** clearly and promptly to **relevant people**

h) your records regarding health and safety and the **work environment** are complete, accurate and comply with organisational and legal requirements.

Knowledge requirements

You need to know and understand

Analytical techniques
- the principles of risk assessment and how to ensure that the work environment is effectively monitored
- how to assess current working conditions and identify possible areas for improvement

Communication
- how to communicate effectively with team members, colleagues, line managers and people outside your organisation

Health and safety
- the importance of health and safety at work and your role and responsibility in relation to this
- the organisational and legal requirements for maintaining a healthy, safe and productive work environment
- industrial or professional codes of practice relevant to healthy, safe and productive work environments
- the types of support it may be necessary to provide on health and safety issues and how to provide such support
- how to respond to contradictions between health and safety requirements and organisational constraints

Organisational context
- the procedures to follow in order to recommend improvements in the work environment
- the records which need to be kept and the organisational and legislative requirements for doing so

Workplace organisation
- the types of work environments which are most conducive to productive work.

Evidence requirements

You must prove that you *maintain a healthy, safe and productive work environment* to the National Standard of competence.

To do this, you must provide evidence to convince your assessor that you consistently meet **all** the performance criteria.

Your evidence must be the result of real work activities undertaken by yourself. Evidence from simulated activities is **only** acceptable for performance criterion f) in this element.

You must show evidence that you provide information, support and recommendations to **two** of the following types of **relevant people**
- team members
- colleagues working at your level
- higher-level managers or sponsors
- people outside your organisation.

Your evidence must cover **all** the following features of the **work environment**
- physical environment
- equipment
- materials
- working procedures.

You must, however, convince your assessor that you have the necessary knowledge, understanding and skills to be able to perform competently in respect of **all** types of **relevant people,** listed above.

Manage activities to meet requirements

Element A2.3

Ensure products and services meet quality requirements

Performance criteria

You must ensure that

a) you give opportunities to **relevant people** to monitor the quality of products and services and recommend improvements to the processes involved

b) your monitoring of the quality of products and services is continuous and complies with your organisation's procedures

c) the products and services within your area of responsibility consistently meet your customers' and **organisation's requirements**

d) where products, services and the processes involved do not meet agreed **requirements**, you take prompt and effective action

e) your records relating to the quality of products and services comply with your organisation's procedures.

Knowledge requirements

You need to know and understand

Involvement and motivation
- the importance of empowering team members to make recommendations on quality improvement and efficiency and how to encourage their contributions

Monitoring and evaluation
- how to monitor the quality of work taking place in your area of responsibility

Organisational context
- the standards and organisational requirements which apply to the activities for which you are responsible
- the records which need to be completed and how this should be done
- how to interpret your organisation's policies and determine their implications for quality assurance

Quality management
- the meaning and importance of quality in the management of activities
- the principles and methods of quality assurance
- deficiencies in quality that are likely to occur and the appropriate corrective actions to take.

Evidence requirements

You must prove that you *ensure products and services meet quality requirements* to the National Standard of competence.

To do this, you must provide evidence to convince your assessor that you consistently meet **all** the performance criteria.

Your evidence must be the result of real work activities undertaken by yourself. Evidence from simulated activities is **not** acceptable for this element.

You must show evidence that you provide opportunities for suggestions and make recommendations to **two** of the following types of **relevant people**
- team members
- colleagues working at the same level
- higher-level managers or sponsors
- specialists.

You must also show evidence that you meet **all** the following types of **organisational requirements**
- quality standards
- organisational policies
- organisational objectives.

You must, however, convince your assessor that you have the necessary knowledge, understanding and skills to be able to perform competently in respect of **all** types of **relevant people**, listed above.

Contribute to improvements at work

Unit summary

This unit is about making significant contributions to improving team and organisational performance. It covers making improvements in your own area of responsibility as well as making recommendations for improvements to organisational plans.

This unit contains two elements

A4.1 *Improve work activities*;
A4.2 *Recommend improvements to organisational plans*.

Personal competencies

In performing effectively in this unit, you will show that you

Communicating
- listen actively, ask questions, clarify points and rephrase others' statements to check mutual understanding
- identify the information needs of listeners
- adopt communication styles appropriate to listeners and situations, including selecting an appropriate time and place
- encourage listeners to ask questions or rephrase statements to clarify their understanding

Focusing on results
- actively seek to do things better
- use change as an opportunity for improvement
- establish and communicate high expectations of performance, including setting an example to others
- monitor quality of work and progress against plans

Influencing others
- present yourself positively to others
- create and prepare strategies for influencing others
- use a variety of means to influence others
- understand the culture of the organisation and act to work within it or influence it

Thinking and taking decisions
- use your own experience and evidence from others to identify problems and understand situations
- produce a variety of solutions before taking a decision
- produce your own ideas from experience and practice
- take decisions which are realistic for the situation.

Contribute to improvements at work

Element A4.1

Improve work activities

Performance criteria

You must ensure that

a) you give opportunities to **relevant people** to make recommendations for improvements to work activities

b) your **monitoring** of activities occurs at intervals most likely to identify potential improvements

c) the information you gather on **trends and developments** is relevant, reliable and sufficient to identify potential improvements

d) you present your recommendations for improvements in activities to **relevant people** at an appropriate time

e) you present your plans for implementing change to **relevant people** at an appropriate time, level and pace

f) you confirm **relevant people's** understanding of the implications of the change and their commitment to their role in it

g) your **monitoring** of the change is sufficient to ensure the intended improvements are achieved

h) you report the results of the change to **relevant people** in the agreed format and timescale

i) the quality of the work for which you are responsible continues to meet the agreed standard throughout the period of change.

Knowledge requirements

You need to know and understand

Change management
- how to recommend improvements and how to take and argue an effective case for change
- how to plan for the management of change in a way which minimises adverse effects
- how to identify the broader implications of change for the work of the organisation and its component parts
- the importance of monitoring change and its effects, and how to undertake such monitoring

Communication
- how to communicate effectively with colleagues, line managers and specialists

Continuous improvement
- the importance of continuous improvement in activities and plans to organisational effectiveness and your role and responsibility in relation to this
- how to assess current work activities and identify areas for improvement

Involvement and motivation
- the importance of empowering other staff to make recommendations and methods to encourage them to do so
- how to motivate others to be committed to change

Organisational context
- the internal and external trends which have a bearing on the future improvements.

Evidence requirements

You must prove that you *improve work activities* to the National Standard of competence.

To do this, you must provide evidence to convince your assessor that you consistently meet **all** the performance criteria.

Your evidence must be the result of real work activities undertaken by yourself. Evidence from simulated activities is **not** acceptable for this element.

You must show evidence that your work in this area involves at least **two** of the following types of **relevant people**
- higher-level managers or sponsors
- colleagues working at the same level as yourself
- specialists.

You must also show evidence that you use at least **two** of the following types of **monitoring** methods
- direct observation
- considering oral information
- considering written information.

You must also show evidence that you gather information on **both** of the following types of **trends and developments**
- inside your organisation
- outside your organisation.

You must, however, convince your assessor that you have the necessary knowledge, understanding and skills to be able to perform competently in respect of **all** types of **relevant people** and **monitoring**, listed above.

Contribute to improvements at work

Element A4.2

Recommend improvements to organisational plans

Performance criteria

You must ensure that

a) your **recommendations** for improvements to organisational plans are based on sufficient valid and reliable information

b) your **recommendations** support the achievement of the organisation's mission, aims and objectives

c) you accurately identify and record the implications of the recommended changes

d) you clearly present your **recommendations** to the people in the organisation most likely to act on them

e) you handle the **discussions** relating to **recommendations** positively and constructively.

Knowledge requirements

You need to know and understand

Involvement and motivation
- how to construct and argue an effective case for change, both in writing and orally

Organisational context
- how to proceed if recommendations are at variance with the mission, aims and objectives of your organisation
- your organisation's mission, aims and objectives
- people in your organisation who are likely to act on recommendations

Planning
- the principles of organisational planning and the models which may be used
- the types of information which are required to make reliable recommendations to plans and the planning process
- how to plan within the framework of the organisation's mission, aims and objectives
- how to identify the likely implications of alterations to plans for the organisation

Working relationships
- how to handle discussions, actual and potential disagreements in a positive and constructive manner.

Evidence requirements

You must prove that you *recommend improvements to organisational plans* to the National Standard of competence.

To do this, you must provide evidence to convince your assessor that you consistently meet **all** the performance criteria.

Your evidence must be the result of real work activities undertaken by yourself. Evidence from simulated activities is **not** acceptable for this element.

You must show evidence that you make **both** of the following types of **recommendations**
- spoken
- written.

You must also show evidence of **both** of the following types of **discussions**
- one-to-one
- group meetings.

Develop your own resources

Unit summary

This unit is about developing your own knowledge and skills and managing your time and other resources so that you can meet your objectives.

This unit contains two elements

C2.1 *Develop yourself to improve your performance*
C2.2 *Manage your own time and resources to meet your objectives.*

Personal competencies

In performing effectively in this unit, you will show that you

Acting assertively
- take personal responsibility for making things happen
- say no to unreasonable requests

Communicating
- identify the information needs of listeners
- encourage listeners to ask questions or rephrase statements to clarify their understanding
- modify communication in response to feedback from listeners

Focusing on results
- maintain a focus on objectives
- tackle problems and take advantage of opportunities as they arise
- prioritise objectives and schedule work to make best use of time and resources
- focus personal attention on specific details that are critical to the success of a key event
- set goals that are demanding of self and others

Managing self
- take responsibility for meeting your own learning and development needs
- seek feedback on performance to identify strengths and weaknesses
- learn from your own mistakes and those of others
- change your behaviour where needed as a result of feedback
- reflect systematically on your own performance and modify your behaviour accordingly
- develop yourself to meet the demands of changing situations
- transfer learning from one situation to another

Thinking and taking decisions
- break processes down into tasks and activities
- identify implications, consequences or causal relationships in a situation
- produce a variety of solutions before taking a decision
- take decisions which are realistic for the situation.

Develop your own resources

Element C2.1

Develop yourself to improve your performance

Performance criteria

You must ensure that

a) you assess your performance and identify your development needs at appropriate intervals

b) your **assessment** is based on your current objectives and likely future requirements

c) your **assessment** takes account of the skills you need to work effectively with other team members

d) your plans for personal development are consistent with the needs you have identified and the resources available

e) your plans for personal development contain specific, measurable, realistic and challenging objectives

f) you obtain support from **relevant people** to help you create learning opportunities

g) you undertake development activities which are consistent with your plans for personal development

h) you obtain feedback from **relevant people** and use it to enhance your performance in the future

i) you update your plans for personal development at appropriate intervals.

Knowledge requirements

You need to know and understand

Communication

- the importance of getting feedback from others on your performance and how to encourage, enable and use such feedback in a constructive manner.

Management competence

- the principal skills required for effective managerial performance
- the types of interpersonal skills required for effective team work.

Organisational context

- the current and likely future requirements and standards within your job role and how they correspond to your level of competence as a manager
- appropriate people from whom to get feedback on your performance.

Training and development

- the importance of continuing self-development to managerial competence
- how to assess your own current level of competence
- how to develop a personal action plan for learning and self-development with realistic but challenging objectives
- the types of support which may be available from your team members, colleagues, line managers and specialists
- how to identify the need for support, select an appropriate source and obtain required help
- the types of development activities and their relative advantages and disadvantages to your own situation
- how to assess your personal progress and update your plans accordingly.

Evidence requirements

You must prove that you *develop yourself to improve your performance* to the National Standard of competence.

To do this, you must provide evidence to convince your assessor that you consistently meet **all** the performance criteria.

Your evidence must be the result of real work activities undertaken by yourself. Evidence from simulated activities is **not** acceptable for this element.

You must show evidence that your **assessments** take account of **all** of the following

- work objectives
- personal objectives
- organisational policies and requirements.

You must also show evidence that you obtain support and feedback from **two** of the following types of **relevant people**

- team members
- colleagues working at the same level as yourself
- higher-level managers or sponsors
- specialists.

You must, however, convince your assessor that you have the necessary knowledge, understanding and skills to be able to perform competently in respect of **all** types of **relevant people**, listed above.

Develop your own resources

Element C2.2

Manage your own time and resources to meet your objectives

Performance criteria

You must ensure that

a) your objectives are specific, measurable and achievable within organisational constraints

b) you prioritise your objectives in line with organisational objectives and policies

c) you plan your work activities so that they are consistent with your objectives and your personal resources

d) your estimates of the time you need for activities are realistic and allow for unforeseen circumstances

e) you **delegate** work to others in a way which makes the most efficient use of available time and resources

f) you take decisions as soon as you have sufficient information

g) when you need further information to take decisions, you take prompt and efficient measures to obtain it

h) you minimise unhelpful interruptions to, and digressions from, planned work

i) you regularly review progress and reschedule activities to help achieve your planned objectives.

Knowledge requirements

You need to know and understand

Delegation
- how to delegate work to others and monitor progress.

Information handling
- how to assess how much information is required before an effective decision can be taken
- how to collect and check the validity of the information required for decision-making.

Monitoring and evaluation
- the importance of regular reviews of activity and rescheduling of work to achieve planned objectives.

Planning
- how to set objectives for yourself which are specific, measurable and achievable
- how to plan activities so that they are consistent with known priorities and your own resources
- how to estimate the amount of time required to carry out planned activities
- the kind of contingencies which may occur and how to assess and plan for these.

Time management
- the importance of effective time management to managerial competence
- how to identify and minimise unhelpful interruptions to planned work.

Evidence requirements

You must prove that you *manage your own time and resources to meet your objectives* to the National Standard of competence.

To do this, you must provide evidence to convince your assessor that you consistently meet **all** the performance criteria.

Your evidence must be the result of real work activities undertaken by yourself. Evidence from simulated activities is **not** acceptable for this element.

You must show evidence that you **delegate** to **one** of the following
- team members
- colleagues working at the same level as yourself
- people outside your organisation.

You must, however, convince your assessor that you have the necessary knowledge, understanding and skills to be able to perform competently in respect of **all** types of people to whom you may have to **delegate**, listed above.

Develop productive working relationships

Unit summary

This unit is about developing productive working relationships with your manager, team members and other colleagues in your organisation. It also involves reducing the opportunity for conflict to a minimum and dealing with conflicts when they arise.

This unit contains three elements

C5.1 *Develop the trust and support of colleagues and team members*
C5.2 *Develop the trust and support of your manager*
C5.3 *Minimise interpersonal conflict*.

Personal competencies

	In performing effectively in this unit, you will show that you

Acting assertively
- act in an assured and unhesitating manner when faced with a challenge
- say no to unreasonable requests
- state your own position and views clearly in conflict situations
- maintain your beliefs, commitment and effort in spite of set-backs or opposition

Behaving ethically
- show integrity and fairness in decision-making
- set objectives and create cultures which are ethical
- clearly identify and raise ethical concerns relevant to your organisation
- work towards the resolution of ethical dilemmas based on reasoned approaches

Building teams
- actively build relationships with others
- make time available to support others
- provide feedback designed to improve people's future performance
- show respect for the views and actions of others
- show sensitivity to the needs and feelings of others
- keep others informed about plans and progress

Communicating
- listen actively, ask questions, clarify points and rephrase others' statements to check mutual understanding
- identify the information needs of listeners
- adopt communication styles appropriate to listeners and situations, including selecting an appropriate time and place

Managing self
- accept personal comments or criticism without becoming defensive
- remain calm in difficult or uncertain situations
- handle others' emotions without becoming personally involved in them

Thinking and making decisions
- reconcile and make use of a variety of perspectives when making sense of a situation
- produce your own ideas from experience and practice
- take decisions which are realistic for the situation
- focus on facts, problems and solutions when handling an emotional situation.

Develop productive working relationships

Element C5.1

Develop the trust and support of colleagues and team members

Performance criteria

You must ensure that

a) you consult with **colleagues** and **team members** about proposed activities at appropriate times and in a manner which encourages open, frank discussion

b) you keep **colleagues** and **team members** informed about organisational plans and activities, emerging threats and opportunities

c) you honour the commitments you make to **colleagues** and **team members**

d) you treat **colleagues** and **team members** in a manner which shows your respect for individuals and the need for confidentiality

e) you give **colleagues** and **team members** sufficient support for them to achieve their work objectives

f) you discuss directly with the **colleagues** and **team members** concerned your evaluation of their work and behaviour.

Knowledge requirements

You need to know and understand

Communication

- how to consult with colleagues in a way which encourages open and frank discussions
- how to select communication methods appropriate to the issues and contexts
- the importance of effective communication methods to productive working relationships
- the importance of discussing evaluations of outputs and behaviour at work promptly and directly with those concerned
- how to provide feedback in a way which will lead to a constructive outcome.

Information handling

- the types of information concerning colleagues which you must treat confidentially and procedures to follow to ensure this.

Organisational context

- the organisational plans, activities and emerging threats and opportunities, which are relevant to the work of colleagues and about which they need to be informed.

Providing support

- the support colleagues may require to achieve their objectives and how to provide such support.

Working relationships

- how people work in groups
- the strategies and styles of working which encourage effective working relationships
- the importance of honouring commitments to colleagues
- the importance of showing respect for colleagues and how to do this.

Evidence requirements

You must prove that you *develop the trust and support of colleagues and team members* to the National Standard of competence.

To do this, you must provide evidence to convince your assessor that you consistently meet **all** the performance criteria.

Your evidence must be the result of real work activities undertaken by yourself. Evidence from simulated activities is **not** acceptable for this element.

You must show evidence of gaining the trust and support of **two** of the following types of **colleagues**

- those working at the same level as you
- those working at a higher level than you
- those working at a lower level than you.

You must also show evidence of gaining the trust and support of **one** of the following types of **team members**

- people for whom you have line management responsibility
- people for whom you have functional responsibility.

You must, however, convince your assessor that you have the necessary knowledge, understanding and skills to be able to perform competently in respect of **all** types of **colleagues** and **team members**, listed above.

Unit C5

Develop productive working relationships

Element C5.2

Develop the trust and support of your manager

Performance criteria

You must ensure that

a) you give your **manager** timely and accurate reports on activities, progress, results and achievements

b) you give your **manager** clear and accurate information about emerging threats and opportunities with a degree of urgency appropriate to the situation

c) you consult your **manager** about organisational policies and ways of working at appropriate times

d) your **proposals** for action are clear and realistic

e) you present your **proposals** for action to your **manager** at appropriate times

f) where you have disagreements with your **manager**, you make constructive efforts to resolve these disagreements and maintain a good working relationship.

Knowledge requirements

You need to know and understand

Communication

- the importance of keeping your manager informed of activities, progress, results and achievements and how to do this
- how to develop and present proposals in ways which are realistic, clear and likely to influence your manager positively.

Organisational context

- management structures, lines of accountability and control
- the general responsibilities of your manager
- the decision-making processes within your organisation
- the types of emerging threats and opportunities about which your manager needs to be informed and the degree of urgency attached to these
- the types of organisational policies and ways of working about which you need to consult with your manager and how to do this.

Working relationships

- the strategies and styles of working which encourage effective working relationships
- how to handle disagreements with your manager in a constructive manner.

Evidence requirements

You must prove that you *develop the trust and support of your manager* to the National Standard of competence.

To do this, you must provide evidence to convince your assessor that you consistently meet **all** the performance criteria.

Your evidence must be the result of real work activities undertaken by yourself. Evidence from simulated activities is acceptable **only** for performance criterion f) in this element.

You must show evidence that you gain the support of a **manager** who is **either**

- the person(s) to whom you report **or**
- the organisation or authority to which you report.

You must also show evidence that you present **proposals** in **one** of the following forms

- spoken
- written.

You must, however, convince your assessor that you have the necessary knowledge, understanding and skills to be able to perform competently in respect of **both** types of **manager** and **proposals**, listed above.

Develop productive working relationships

Element C5.3

Minimise interpersonal conflict

Performance criteria

You must ensure that

a) you inform **individuals** of the standards of work and behaviour you expect in a manner, and at a level and pace appropriate to the **individuals** concerned

b) you provide opportunities for **individuals** to discuss **problems** which directly or indirectly affect their work

c) you take action promptly to deal with conflicts between **individuals**

d) you inform **relevant people** about conflicts outside your area of responsibility

e) the ways you resolve conflicts minimise disruption to work and discord between **individuals**

f) the way you resolve conflict complies with organisational and legal requirements

g) your records of conflicts and their outcomes are accurate, and comply with requirements for confidentiality and other organisational policies

h) you make recommendations for improving procedures and reducing the potential for conflict promptly to the **relevant people**.

Knowledge requirements

You need to know and understand

Communication

- how to recommend improvements in the way your organisation tries to reduce conflict.

Information handling

- the importance of maintaining accurate records of conflicts and their outcomes
- the information regarding conflicts which must be treated confidentially and the people who may and may not be informed.

Organisational context

- the people to inform when conflicts are outside your area of responsibility
- the organisational requirements regarding the handling of conflict and its resolution.

Working relationships

- the situations, behaviour and interactions between people which encourage conflict
- how to minimise conflict between people at work
- the importance of keeping people regularly informed of expected standards of work and behaviour
- how to inform people of the standards and behaviour you expect
- the importance of giving people opportunities to discuss problems affecting their work and how to do this
- how to identify potential conflict between individuals in your organisation
- the types of conflict which may occur between people at work and action to take in response to these which will minimise disruption to work.

Evidence requirements

You must prove that you *minimise interpersonal conflict* to the National Standard of competence.

To do this, you must provide evidence to convince your assessor that you consistently meet **all** the performance criteria.

Your evidence must be the result of real work activities undertaken by yourself. Evidence from simulated activities is acceptable **only** for performance criteria c)–g) in this element.

You must show evidence of minimising conflict between **one** of the following types of **individuals**

- team members
- colleagues working at the same level as you
- colleagues working at a lower level than you.

You must show evidence of discussing **problems** which are **either**

- work-related **or**
- personal.

You must also show evidence of making recommendations to **one** of the following types of **relevant people**

- higher-level managers or sponsors
- colleagues working at the same level as yourself
- specialists.

You must, however, convince your assessor that you have the necessary knowledge, understanding and skills to be able to perform competently in respect of **all** types of **individuals**, **problems** and **relevant people**, listed above.

Provide information to support decision making

Unit summary

This unit is about providing information so that sound decisions can be taken. It covers obtaining relevant information, recording and storing this information, and analysing this information so that decisions can be taken. It also covers advising and informing other people.

This unit contains four elements

D4.1   *Obtain information for decision making*
D4.2   *Record and store information*
D4.3   *Analyse information to support decision making*
D4.4   *Advise and inform others.*

Personal competencies

In performing effectively in this unit, you will show that you

Communicating
- listen actively, ask questions, clarify points and rephrase others' statements to check mutual understanding
- adopt communication styles appropriate to listeners and situations, including selecting an appropriate time and place
- encourage listeners to ask questions or rephrase statements to clarify their understanding

Influencing others
- present yourself positively to others
- create and prepare strategies for influencing others
- use a variety of means to influence others
- understand the culture of your organisation and act to work within it or influence it

Searching for information
- establish information networks to search for and gather relevant information
- make best use of existing sources of information
- seek information from multiple sources
- challenge the validity and reliability of sources of information
- push for concrete information in an ambiguous situation

Thinking and taking decisions
- break processes down into tasks and activities
- use your own experience and evidence from others to identify problems and understand situations
- identify patterns or meaning from events and data which are not obviously related
- produce a variety of solutions before taking a decision
- produce your own ideas from experience and practice
- take decisions which are realistic for the situation.

Provide information to support
decision making

Element D4.1

Obtain information for decision making

Performance criteria

You must ensure that

a) you identify the **information** you need to make the required decisions

b) the **sources** of **information** which you use are reliable and sufficiently wide-ranging to meet current and likely future **information** requirements

c) your **methods** of obtaining **information** are reliable, effective and make efficient use of resources

d) your **methods** of obtaining **information** are consistent with organisational values, policies and legal requirements

e) the **information** you obtain is accurate, relevant and sufficient to support decision making

f) where **information** is inadequate, contradictory or ambiguous, you take prompt and effective action to deal with this.

Knowledge requirements

You need to know and understand

Analytical techniques

- how to judge the accuracy, relevance and sufficiency of information required to support decision making in different contexts
- how to identify information which may be contradictory, ambiguous or inadequate and how to deal with these problems

Information handling

- the importance of information management to the team and organisational effectiveness and your role and responsibilities in relation to this
- the types of qualitative and quantitative information which are essential to your role and responsibilities, and how to identify these
- the range of sources of information which are available to you and how to ensure that these are capable of meeting current and likely future information requirements
- how to identify new sources of information which may be required
- the range of methods of gathering and checking the validity of such information and their advantages and disadvantages

Organisational context

- the organisational values and policies and the legal requirements which have a bearing on the collection of information and how to interpret these.

Evidence requirements

You must prove that you *obtain information for decision making* to the National Standard of competence.

To do this, you must provide evidence to convince your assessor that you consistently meet **all** the performance criteria.

Your evidence must be the result of real work activities undertaken by yourself. Evidence from simulated activities is **not** acceptable for this element.

You must show evidence that you use at least **three** of the following types of **sources** of information

- people within your organisation
- people outside your organisation
- internal information systems
- published media
- specially commissioned research.

You must also show evidence that you obtain **both** of the following types of **information**

- quantitative
- qualitative.

You must also show evidence that you use **four** of the following types of **methods** of obtaining information

- listening and watching
- reading
- spoken questioning
- written questioning
- formal research conducted personally
- formal research conducted by third parties.

You must, however, convince your assessor that you have the necessary knowledge, understanding and skills to be able to perform competently in respect of **all** types of **sources** of information and **methods** of obtaining information listed above.

Provide information to support
decision making

Element D4.2

Record and store information

Performance criteria

You must ensure that

a) your **systems and procedures** for recording and storing **information** are suitable for the purpose and make efficient use of resources

b) the way you record and store **information** complies with organisational policies and legal requirements

c) the **information** you record and store is readily accessible in the required format to authorised people only

d) you provide opportunities for team members to make suggestions for improvements to **systems and procedures**

e) you make recommendations for improvements to **systems and procedures** to the relevant people

f) your recommendations take account of **organisational constraints**.

Knowledge requirements

You need to know and understand

Communication
- different formats which may be required for presenting qualitative and quantitative information
- how to select a format appropriate to different purposes and recipients of information

Continuous improvement
- how to assess the effectiveness of current methods of collecting and storing information and the procedures to follow in order to make recommendations on improvements

Information handling
- different methods of recording and storing information and their advantages and disadvantages
- how to ensure that information is organised in a way that makes it readily accessible
- principles of confidentiality – what information should be made available to which people

Involvement and motivation
- the importance of providing opportunities for team members to make recommendations on improvements to systems and procedures
- how to encourage and enable team members to make recommendation

Organisational context
- the organisational policies and legal requirements which have a bearing on the recording and storage of information and how to interpret these.

Evidence requirements

You must prove that you *record and store information* to the National Standard of competence.

To do this, you must provide evidence to convince your assessor that you consistently meet **all** the performance criteria.

Your evidence must be the result of real work activities undertaken by yourself. Evidence from simulated activities is **not** acceptable for this element.

You must show evidence that you use **one** of the following types of **systems and procedures**
- organisation wide
- specific to yourself and your team.

You must show evidence that you record and store **both** of the following types of **information**
- quantitative
- qualitative.

You must also show evidence that you take account of **all** the following types of **organisational constraints**
- organisational objectives
- organisational policies
- resources.

You must, however, convince your assessor that you have the necessary knowledge, understanding and skills to be able to perform competently in respect of **all** types of **systems and procedures** listed above.

Provide information to support
decision making

Element D4.3

Analyse
information
to support
decision making

Performance criteria

You must ensure that

a) you identify objectives for your **analysis**
   which are clear and consistent with the
   decisions which need to be made

b) you select **information** which is
   accurate, relevant to the objectives, and
   sufficient to arrive at reliable **decisions**

c) you use methods of **analysis** which are
   suitable to achieve the objectives

d) your **analysis** of the **information**
   correctly identifies relevant patterns and
   trends

e) you support your conclusions with
   reasoned argument and appropriate
   evidence

f) in presenting the results of your
   analysis you differentiate clearly
   between fact and opinion

g) your records of the **analysis** are
   sufficient to show the assumptions and
   decisions made at each stage.

Knowledge requirements

You need to know and understand

Analytical techniques
- different approaches to, and methods of, analysing information and how to select methods appropriate to decisions which you have to make
- how to analyse information to identify patterns and trends
- how to draw conclusions on the basis of analysing information
- the differences between fact and opinion, how to identify these and present them accordingly

Communication
- how to develop and present a reasoned case based on the outcomes of an analysis

Information handling
- the importance of the effective analysis of information; your role and responsibility in relation to this
- types of information, both qualitative and quantitative, which you need to able to analyse
- how to select information relevant to the decisions you need to make and ensure such information is accurate and relevant
- the importance of record-keeping to the analysis of information and how such records should be kept and used.

Evidence requirements

You must prove that you *analyse information to support decision making* to the National Standard of competence.

To do this, you must provide evidence to convince your assessor that you consistently meet **all** the performance criteria.

Your evidence must be the result of real work activities undertaken by yourself. Evidence from simulated activities is **not** acceptable for this element.

You must show evidence that you carry out **both** of the following types of **analysis**
- formal and planned
- informal and ad hoc.

You must show evidence that your analysis supports **decisions** concerning **both** of the following
- day-to-day operations
- changes in organisational policy which affect operations.

You must also show evidence that you use **both** of the following types of **information**
- qualitative
- quantitative.

Provide information to support decision making

Element D4.4

Advise and inform others

Performance criteria

You must ensure that

a) you research the **advice and information** needs of your **recipients** in ways which are appropriate and sufficient and takes account of your **organisational constraints**

b) you provide **advice and information** at a time and place and in a **form** and manner appropriate to the needs of your **recipients**

c) the **information** you provide is accurate, current, relevant and sufficient

d) your **advice** is consistent with organisational policy, procedures and **constraints**

e) your **advice** is supported by reasoned argument and appropriate evidence

f) you confirm your **recipients'** understanding of the **advice and information** you have given

g) you maintain confidentiality according to organisational and legal requirements

h) you use feedback from **recipients** to improve the way you provide **advice and information**.

Knowledge requirements

You need to know and understand

Communication

- how to communicate advice and information effectively both through speaking and in writing
- how to develop and present a reasoned case when providing advice to others
- the importance of confirming the recipient's understanding of information and advice provided and how to do this
- the importance of providing advice and information and your role and responsibilities in relation to this
- the types of advice and information which people may require
- how to identify information needs
- situations in which it is appropriate to act on one's own initiative in giving information and advice
- the importance of seeking feedback on the quality and relevance of the advice and information you provide and how to encourage such feedback

Information handling

- the importance of checking the validity of advice and information provided to others
- how to ensure accuracy, currency, sufficiency and relevance of advice and information
- the principles of confidentiality when handling information and advice – what types of information and advice may be provided to what people

Organisational context

- organisational policies, procedures and resource constraints which may affect advice given to others

Evidence requirements

You must prove that you *advise and inform others* to the National Standard of competence.

To do this, you must provide evidence to convince your assessor that you consistently meet **all** the performance criteria.

Your evidence must be the result of real work activities undertaken by yourself. Evidence from simulated activities is **not** acceptable for this element.

You must show evidence that you provide **both** of the following **forms** of advice and information

- spoken
- written.

You must show evidence that you provide **advice and information** in **both** of the following circumstances

- in response to a request
- on your own initiative.

You must show evidence that you provide information and advice to at least **two** of the following types of **recipients**

- team members
- colleagues working at the same level
- higher-level managers and sponsors
- people outside your organisation.

You must also show evidence that you take account of **all** of the following types of **organisational constraints**

- organisational objectives
- organisational policies
- resources.

You must, however, convince your assessor that you have the necessary knowledge, understanding and skills to be able to perform competently in respect of **all** types of **recipients** listed above.

Manage the use of physical resources

Unit summary

This unit is about efficiently managing the physical resources for which you are responsible. It covers planning to use the resources you and your team need, obtaining those resources, ensuring the availability of suitable supplies, and monitoring the use of resources.

This unit contains four elements

B2.1 *Plan the use of physical resources*
B2.2 *Obtain physical resources*
B2.3 *Ensure availability of supplies*
B2.4 *Monitor the use of physical resources.*

Personal competencies

In performing effectively in this unit, you will show that you

Communicating
- listen actively, ask questions, clarify points and rephrase others' statements to check mutual understanding
- identify the information needs of listeners
- adopt communications styles appropriate to listeners and situations, including selecting an appropriate time and place

Focusing on results
- maintain a focus on objectives
- tackle problems and take advantage of opportunities as they arise
- prioritise objectives and schedule work to make best use of time and resources
- monitor quality of work and progress against plans

Influencing others
- develop and use contacts to trade information, and obtain support and resources
- present yourself positively to others
- create and prepare strategies for influencing others
- use a variety of means to influence others
- understand the culture of your organisation and act to work within it or influence it

Thinking and taking decisions
- break processes down into tasks and activities
- identify a range of elements in and perspectives on a situation
- identify implications, consequences or causal relationships in a situation
- use your own experience and evidence from others to identify problems and understand situations
- produce a variety of solutions before taking a decision
- take decisions which are realistic for the situation.

Manage the use of physical
resources

Element B2.1

Plan the use of physical resources

Performance criteria

You must ensure that

a) you give opportunities to **relevant people** to provide information about the physical resources required

b) your **plans** take account of relevant past experience, trends and developments and factors likely to affect future resource use

c) your **plans** are consistent with your organisation's objectives, policies and legal requirements

d) you present your **plans** to **relevant people** in an appropriate and timely manner.

Knowledge requirements

You need to know and understand

Communication
- how to present and communicate plans on resource usage effectively

Involvement and motivation
- how to encourage and enable staff to communicate their needs for resources

Organisational context
- organisational objectives, policies and legal requirements relevant to resource usage, how to interpret these and identify the implications for resource planning

Planning
- the principles underpinning effective resource planning and your role and responsibility in relation to this
- how to develop short-, medium- and long-term plans for the use of resources
- the types of trends and developments which might impact on your use of resources, how to analyse these and draw out the implications for planning.

Evidence requirements

You must prove that you *plan the use of physical resources* to the National Standard of competence.

To do this, you must provide evidence to convince your assessor that you consistently meet **all** the performance criteria.

Your evidence must be the result of real work activities undertaken by yourself. Evidence from simulated activities is **not** acceptable for this element.

You must show evidence that you seek information from, and present plans to, at least **two** types of the following **relevant people**
- team members
- colleagues working at the same level
- higher-level managers or sponsors
- people outside your organisation.

You must also show evidence of **two** of the following types of **plans**
- short term
- medium term
- long term.

You must, however, convince your assessor that you have the necessary knowledge, understanding and skills to be able to perform competently in respect of **all** types of **relevant people** and **plans**, listed above.

Manage the use of physical resources

Obtain physical resources

Performance criteria

You must ensure that

a) your **requests** for physical resources clearly show the costs involved and the anticipated benefits you expect from the use of the resources

b) you present your **requests** for physical resources to **relevant people** in time for the necessary resources to be obtained

c) you present **requests** for physical resources in ways which reflect the commitment of those who will be using the resources

d) the physical resources you obtain are sufficient to support all activities within your control

e) where you cannot obtain the physical resources you need in full, you agree appropriate amendments to your plans with **relevant people**.

Knowledge requirements

You need to know and understand

Analytical techniques
- how to carry out cost-benefit analyses for the use of resources

Communication
- how to develop and present an effective case for resources to relevant people

Involvement and motivation
- how to obtain and maximise commitment to resource planning

Organisational context
- procedures to follow in order to request resources

Planning
- how to adjust work plans in the event of required resources not being available

Resource management
- the physical resources which you need to carry out your activities effectively.

Evidence requirements

You must prove that you *obtain physical resources* to the National Standard of competence.

To do this, you must provide evidence to convince your assessor that you consistently meet **all** the performance criteria.

Your evidence must be the result of real work activities undertaken by yourself. Evidence from simulated activities is **not** acceptable for this element.

You must show evidence that you make **both** of the following types of **requests**
- spoken
- written.

You must show evidence that you can make and agree amendments to your plans with **two** of the following types of **relevant people**
- team members
- colleagues working at the same level as yourself
- higher-level managers or sponsors
- people outside your organisation.

You must, however, convince your assessor that you have the necessary knowledge, understanding and skills to be able to perform competently in respect of **all** types of **relevant people**, listed above.

Manage the use of physical resources

Ensure availability of supplies

Performance criteria

You must ensure that

a) you identify the **supplies** you need accurately

b) the range of **suppliers** from which you choose is sufficiently wide to ensure adequate competition and continuity of **supplies**

c) you negotiate with **suppliers** in a manner which will maintain good relations with them

d) the agreements you reach with **suppliers** provide good value and comply with organisational and legal requirements

e) you **monitor** the quality and quantity of **supplies** at appropriate intervals

f) the **supplies** you obtain consistently meet your organisation's requirements for quality, quantity and delivery

g) you deal with any actual or potential problems with **supplies** promptly

h) your records of **supplies** are complete, accurate and available only to authorised people.

Knowledge requirements

You need to know and understand

Agreements and contracts
- how to establish effective agreements with suppliers and the legal, ethical and organisational requirements which govern these

Analytical techniques
- how to analyse work activities to identify required supplies
- how to select from a range of suppliers to ensure value for money, consistency, quality and continuity of supply within organisational and legal requirements

Monitoring and evaluation
- how to monitor the provision of supplies to ensure ongoing quality, quantity, delivery and time requirements are being met

Organisational context
- the legal and organisational requirements which govern the selection of suppliers, how to interpret these and identify the implications for your work

Resource management
- the importance of continuity of supplies to maintaining the quality of products and services and your role and responsibility in relation to this
- the range of suppliers available for the physical resources you require
- the range of problems which may occur with supplies and suppliers and effective corrective action to take in response to these
- the importance of accurate record-keeping in managing supplies and suppliers, and systems to ensure that this happens properly.

Evidence requirements

You must prove that you *ensure availability of supplies* to the National Standard of competence.

To do this, you must provide evidence to convince your assessor that you consistently meet **all** the performance criteria.

Your evidence must be the result of real work activities undertaken by yourself. Evidence from simulated activities is **not** acceptable for this element.

You must show evidence that you obtain **one** of the following types of **supplies**
- goods
- services.

You must show evidence that you work with **one** of the following types of **suppliers**
- those inside your organisation
- those outside your organisation.

You must show evidence that you use **two** of the following types of **monitoring**
- direct observation
- considering oral information from others
- considering written information from others.

You must, however, convince your assessor that you have the necessary knowledge, understanding and skills to be able to perform competently in respect of **all** types of **supplies**, **suppliers** and **monitoring**, listed above.

Manage the use of physical resources

Element B2.4

Monitor the use of physical resources

Performance criteria

You must ensure that

a) you give opportunities to team members to take individual responsibility for the efficient use of physical resources

b) your team's use of physical resources is efficient and takes into account the possible impact on the environment

c) you **monitor** the quality of physical resources continuously

d) your methods of **monitoring** the use of physical resources are reliable and comply with organisational requirements

e) you **monitor** the actual use of physical resources against an agreed plan at appropriate intervals

f) you take prompt **corrective action** to deal with actual or potential significant deviations from your plan

g) your records relating to the use of physical resources are complete, accurate and available to authorised people only.

Knowledge requirements

You need to know and understand

Information handling
- principles of confidentiality regarding the use of resources: which types of information may be made available to whom

Involvement and motivation
- how to encourage and empower team members to take responsibility for the efficient use of resources

Monitoring and evaluation
- the importance of effective monitoring of resource use to organisational efficiency and your role and responsibility in relation to this
- how to monitor and control resource usage to maintain consistency and quality in the provision of products and services

Organisational context
- the organisational and legal requirements regarding the impact of resource usage on the environment and how to minimise adverse effects
- your organisation's requirements for controlling resource usage
- your planned objectives and measures for resource usage

Resource management
- the range of obstacles to efficient use of resources and effective corrective action to take in response to these
- the importance of effective record keeping in the use of resources and how to ensure that this happens.

Evidence requirements

You must prove that you *monitor the use of physical resources* to the National Standard of competence.

To do this, you must provide evidence to convince your assessor that you consistently meet **all** the performance criteria.

Your evidence must be the result of real work activities undertaken by yourself. Evidence from simulated activities is **not** acceptable for this element.

You must show evidence that you use **two** of the following types of **monitoring**
- your own observation
- considering oral information from others
- considering written information from others.

You must also show evidence that you can take at least **two** of the following types of **corrective action**
- altering activities
- modifying the use of physical resources for activities
- renegotiating the allocation of physical resources.

You must, however, convince your assessor that you have the necessary knowledge, understanding and skills to be able to perform competently in respect of **all** types of **monitoring** and **corrective action**, listed above.

Manage the use of financial resources

Unit summary

This unit is about making sure you use financial resources in the most efficient way possible. It covers making recommendations for the use of financial resources and controlling expenditure against budgets.

This unit contains two elements

B3.1 *Make recommendations for expenditure*
B3.2 *Control expenditure against budgets.*

Personal competencies

In performing effectively in this unit, you will show that you

Acting assertively
- take personal responsibility for making things happen
- act in an assured and unhesitating manner when faced with a challenge
- say no to unreasonable requests
- state your own position and views clearly in conflict situations

Communicating
- listen actively, ask questions, clarify points and rephrase others' statements and check mutual understanding
- adopt communication styles appropriate to listeners and situations, including selecting an appropriate time and place
- present difficult ideas and problems in ways that promote understanding

Influencing others
- present yourself positively to others
- create and prepare strategies for influencing others
- understand the culture of your organisation and act to work within it or influence it

Focusing on results
- establish and communicate high expectations of performance, including setting an example to others
- set goals that are demanding of self and others

Searching for information
- make best use of existing sources of information
- seek information from multiple sources
- actively encourage the free exchange of information
- challenge the validity and reliability of sources of information

Thinking and taking decisions
- break processes down into tasks and activities
- use your own experience and evidence from others to identify problems and understand situations
- produce a variety of solutions before taking a decision
- take decisions which are realistic for the situation.

Manage the use of financial resources

Element B3.1

Make recommendations for expenditure

Performance criteria

You must ensure that

a) you give opportunities to **relevant people** to make suggestions for future **expenditure**

b) your recommendations take account of past experience, trends, developments and other factors likely to affect future **expenditure**

c) you clearly state the expected benefits from the recommended **expenditure**, and any potential negative consequences

d) where you have considered **alternative options** for **expenditure**, you provide valid reasons why you have rejected them

e) you provide sufficient, valid information for **relevant people** to make a decision on your recommendations

f) your recommendations for **expenditure** are consistent with your organisation's plans and objectives

g) you present your recommendations to **relevant people** in an appropriate format and at an appropriate time.

Knowledge requirements

You need to know and understand

Analytical techniques

- how to analyse expenditure in the past and use the results to make recommendations on more effective use of financial resources in the future
- how to carry out cost-benefit analyses in regard to proposed expenditure
- how to identify and evaluate alternative options to proposals on expenditure

Communication

- how to communicate effectively on issues to do with proposed expenditure

Involvement and motivation

- how to enable team members, colleagues and line managers to identify and communicate their needs regarding expenditure
- how to develop and argue an effective case for expenditure

Organisational context

- the trends and developments which may influence future expenditure and how to forecast and plan for these
- the procedures which need to be followed to make recommendations for expenditure

Resource management

- the importance of effective budgetary control to team and organisational efficiency and your role and responsibilities in relation to this
- the principles and methods which underpin effective budgetary control
- the importance of keeping accurate records of past expenditure
- the information which others need to make decisions on expenditure and how to gather and check the validity of this information.

Evidence requirements

You must prove that you *make recommendations for expenditure* to the National Standard of competence.

To do this, you must provide evidence to convince your assessor that you consistently meet **all** the performance criteria.

Your evidence must be the result of real work-activities undertaken by yourself. Evidence from simulated activities is **not** acceptable for this element.

You must show evidence that you involve at least **two** of the following types of **relevant people**

- team members
- colleagues working at the same level
- higher-level managers or sponsors
- financial specialists.

You must show evidence that your recommendations cover at least **two** of the following types of **expenditure**

- supplies
- people
- overhead expenses
- capital equipment.

You must also show evidence that you consider at least **both** of the following types of **alternative options**

- other courses of action to achieve the same results
- other ways of funding the same course of actions.

You must, however, convince your assessor that you have the necessary knowledge, understanding and skills to be able to perform competently in respect of **all** types of **relevant people** and **expenditure**, listed above.

Manage the use of financial resources

Element B3.2

Control expenditure against budgets

Performance criteria

You must ensure that

a) you give team members clear and consistent advice on how they can help to control **expenditure**

b) you give team members opportunities to take individual responsibility for **monitoring** and controlling **expenditure**

c) your methods of **monitoring expenditure** are reliable and comply with organisational requirements

d) you **monitor expenditure** against agreed budgets at appropriate intervals

e) you control **expenditure** in line with budgets and organisational requirements

f) the **corrective action** you take in response to actual or potential significant variations from budget is prompt and complies with organisational requirements

g) you refer requests for **expenditure** outside your responsibility promptly to the appropriate people

h) your records of **expenditure** are complete, accurate and available to authorised people only.

Knowledge requirements

You need to know and understand

Information handling

the principles of confidentiality in relation to budgets – what information may be provided to which people

Involvement and motivation

the contributions your team members can make to expenditure control

how to advise, encourage and motivate team members to help in controlling expenditure

Organisational context

your organisation's requirements for expenditure control

the range of variations from the budget which may occur and what effective corrective action to take in response to these

the types of requests for expenditure outside your control which are likely to occur and the correct procedures to follow in response to these

Resource management

the importance of effective expenditure control to your team and organisation's efficiency and your role and responsibilities in relation to this

the principles and systems which underpin effective expenditure control

the importance of accurate and comprehensive record-keeping to expenditure control and systems to achieve this.

Evidence requirements

You must prove that you *control expenditure against budgets* to the National Standard of competence.

To do this, you must provide evidence to convince your assessor that you consistently meet **all** the performance criteria.

Your evidence must be the result of real work activities undertaken by yourself. Evidence from simulated activities is **not** acceptable for this element.

You must show evidence that you use at least **two** of the following types of **monitoring**

- by considering oral information
- by considering written information
- by examining financial information.

You must show evidence that you control at least **two** of the following types of **expenditure**

- supplies
- people
- overhead expenses
- capital equipment.

You must also show evidence that you take at least **two** of the following types of **corrective action**

- altering activities
- rescheduling expenditure
- altering budget allocations within the limits of your responsibility
- renegotiating budgets.

You must, however, convince your assessor that you have the necessary knowledge, understanding and skills to be able to perform competently in respect of **all** types of **monitoring**, **expenditure** and **corrective action**, listed above.

Management

Level 4

NVQ/SVQ

Optional units
Candidates take THREE optional units

Select personnel for activities

Unit summary

This unit is about recruiting and selecting the people you need to carry out your work activities. It applies to both external and internal recruitment of people for permanent work, temporary work or project work. It applies equally to paid or voluntary work, whether full-time or part-time.

This unit contains two elements

C8.1 *Identify personnel requirements*
C8.2 *Select required personnel.*

Personal competencies

In performing effectively in this unit, you will show that you

Acting assertively	• state your own position and views clearly in conflict situations • maintain your own beliefs, commitment and effort in spite of set-backs and opposition
Behaving ethically	• comply with legislation, industry regulation, professional and organisational codes • show integrity and fairness in decision-making
Communicating	• listen actively, ask questions, clarify points and rephrase others' statements and check mutual understanding • adopt communication styles appropriate to listeners and situations, including selecting an appropriate time and place • confirm listeners' understanding through questioning and interpretation of non-verbal signals • encourage listeners to ask questions or rephrase statements to clarify their understanding • modify communication in response to feedback from listeners
Influencing others	• present yourself positively to others • create and prepare strategies for influencing others • understand the culture of your organisation and act to work within it or influence it
Searching for information	• actively encourage the free exchange of information • make best use of existing sources of information • seek information from multiple sources • challenge the validity and reliability of sources of information • push for concrete information in an ambiguous situation
Thinking and taking decisions	• break processes down into tasks and activities • identify patterns or meaning from events and data which are not obviously related • take decisions which are realistic for the situation.

Select personnel for activities

Element C8.1

Identify personnel requirements

Performance criteria

You must ensure that

a) you clearly and accurately identify the organisational objectives and constraints affecting **personnel** requirements

b) you consult with relevant people on **personnel** requirements in a timely and confidential manner

c) your estimates of **personnel** requirements are based on an accurate analysis of sufficient, up-to-date and reliable information

d) the **specifications** you develop are clear, accurate and comply with organisational and legal requirements

e) the **specifications** you develop identify fair and objective criteria for selection

f) the **specifications** you develop are agreed with **authorised people** prior to recruitment action.

Knowledge requirements

You need to know and understand

Communication
- how to make a case for additional personnel requirements in a way which is likely to influence decision-makers positively.

Information handling
- how to collect and validate the information needed to specify personnel requirements.

Involvement and motivation
- the issues for which consultation with relevant people may be necessary and how to do so
- the importance of agreeing personnel requirements in advance with relevant people.

Legal requirements
- the legal requirements for the specification of personnel requirements.

Organisational context
- the work objectives and constraints which have a bearing on identifying personnel requirements.

Recruitment and selection
- the methods of specifying personnel requirements and their relative advantages and disadvantages to your work
- how to identify personnel needs for your team and specify job roles, competences and attributes required to meet these needs
- the types of information necessary to specify personnel requirements
- how to identify fair and objective criteria for the selection of staff.

Evidence requirements

You must prove that you *identify personnel requirements* to the National Standard of competence.

To do this, you must provide evidence to convince your assessor that you consistently meet **all** the performance criteria.

Your evidence must be the result of real work activities undertaken by yourself. Evidence from simulated activities is **not** acceptable for this element.

You must show evidence that you identify requirements for at least **four** of the following types of **personnel**
- internal
- permanent
- full-time
- paid
- external
- temporary
- part-time
- voluntary.

You must also show evidence that you involve at least **two** of the following types of **authorised people**
- team members
- colleagues working at the same level as yourself
- higher-level managers or sponsors
- personnel specialists
- members of the selection team.

You must also show evidence that you develop **all** of the following types of **specifications**
- key purpose of the posts
- individual and team roles and responsibilities
- required individual and team competencies
- other details specific to the organisation.

You must, however, convince your assessor that you have the necessary knowledge, understanding and skills to be able to perform competently in respect of **all** types of **personnel** and **authorised people**, listed above.

Select personnel for activities

Element C8.2

Select required personnel

Performance criteria

You must ensure that

a) you use appropriately skilled and experienced people to assess and select **personnel**

b) the **information** you obtain about each candidate is relevant to and sufficient for the selection process

c) you assess the **information** objectively against specified selection criteria

d) your selection decisions are justifiable from the evidence gained

e) you only inform authorised people about selection decisions and the identified development needs of successful candidates

f) the **information** you provide to authorised people is clear and accurate

g) all candidates receive feedback and **information** appropriate to their needs at each stage of the selection process

h) your records of the selection process are complete, accurate, clear and comply with organisational and legal requirements

i) you pass on your recommendations for improvements to the selection process to the appropriate people in your organisation.

Knowledge requirements

You need to know and understand

Communication
- how to present and justify selection decisions
- how to communicate selection decisions.

Continuous improvement
- the importance of continually reviewing your selection processes and how to do so
- how to make a case for change in selection processes.

Information handling
- the importance of confidentiality during the selection process
- the importance of accurate record-keeping during the selection process.

Legal requirements
- the legal requirements for the selection of personnel

Organisational context
- the organisational requirements for the selection of personnel.

Recruitment and selection
- the relative advantages and disadvantages of the range of methods which may be used for the assessment and selection of staff to your work
- the skills and experience staff need to take part in selection processes
- the information you need to select personnel
- how to make fair and objective assessments
- how to identify the additional development needs of those you select and what to do with this information
- why all candidates should receive feedback at appropriate points during the selection process.

Evidence requirements

You must prove that you *select required personnel* to the National Standard of competence.

To do this, you must provide evidence to convince your assessor that you consistently meet **all** the performance criteria.

Your evidence must be the result of real work activities undertaken by yourself. Evidence from simulated activities is **not** acceptable for this element.

You must show evidence that you select at least **four** of the following types of **personnel**
- internal
- external
- permanent
- temporary
- full-time
- part-time
- paid
- voluntary.

You must also show evidence that you obtain and assess at least **four** of the following types of **information**
- biographical data
- letters
- references
- interview responses
- presentations
- results of work skill tests
- results of knowledge tests.

You must, however, convince your assessor that you have the necessary knowledge, understanding and skills to be able to perform competently in respect of **all** types of **personnel** and **information**, listed above.

Develop teams and individuals to enhance performance

Unit summary

This unit is about developing your team's skills and knowledge to ensure the best possible results at work. It covers identifying the development needs of your team and its members, planning their development and using a variety of activities to improve team performance. It also covers your role in supporting individuals' learning, assessing teams and individuals against agreed development objectives, and continually improving development activities, policies and overall practice.

This unit contains six elements

C10.1 *Identify the development needs of teams and individuals*
C10.2 *Plan the development of teams and individuals*
C10.3 *Develop teams to improve performance*
C10.4 *Support individual learning and development*
C10.5 *Assess the development of teams and individuals*
C10.6 *Improve the development of teams and individuals.*

Personal competencies

In performing effectively in this unit, you will show that you

Acting assertively
- state your own position and views clearly in conflict situations
- maintain your beliefs, commitment and effort in spite of set-backs or opposition

Building teams
- make time available to support others
- encourage and stimulate others to make the best use of their abilities
- evaluate and enhance people's capability to do their jobs
- provide feedback designed to improve people's future performance
- use power and authority in a fair and equitable manner
- invite others to contribute to planning and organising work
- set objectives which are both achievable and challenging

Communicating
- listen actively, ask questions, clarify points and rephrase others' statements to check mutual understanding
- identify the information needs of listeners
- adopt communication styles appropriate to listeners and situations, including selecting an appropriate time and place
- use a variety of media and communication aids to reinforce points and maintain interest
- present difficult ideas and problems in ways that promote understanding
- confirm listeners' understanding through questioning and interpretation of non-verbal signals
- encourage listeners to ask questions or rephrase statements to clarify their understanding
- modify communication in response to feedback from listeners

Thinking and taking decisions
- break processes down into tasks and activities
- use your own experience and evidence from others to identify problems and understand situations
- take decisions which are realistic for the situation.

Develop teams and individuals to enhance performance

Identify the development needs of teams and individuals

Performance criteria

You must ensure that

a) you give opportunities to team members to help identify their own **development needs** and those of the team as a whole

b) you identify **development needs** accurately and base your decisions on sufficient reliable and valid information

c) you identify **development needs** for all the **personnel** you are responsible for

d) where required, you seek guidance from competent **specialists**

e) you provide information on **development needs** to authorised people only, in the format required and to agreed deadlines

f) your records of identified **development needs** comply with organisational procedures.

Knowledge requirements

You need to know and understand

Communication

- how to present development needs to relevant people in a way which is likely to influence their decision-making positively.

Continuous improvement

- the importance of human resource development to organisational effectiveness.

Equal opportunities

- the importance of equality of opportunity in human resource development.

Information handling

- how to collect and validate the information you need to identify development needs
- the importance of good record-keeping.

Involvement and motivation

- the importance of providing your team members with opportunities to identify their own development needs and those of the team as a whole
- how to encourage and enable team members to identify development needs.

Organisational context

- the team objectives and organisational values which have a bearing on the identification of training needs.

Training and development

- how to identify development needs for your team and the information needed to do so
- the types of support and guidance which may be needed from specialists and how to get them.

Evidence requirements

You must prove that you *identify the development needs of teams and individuals* to the National Standard of competence.

To do this, you must provide evidence to convince your assessor that you consistently meet **all** the performance criteria.

Your evidence must be the result of real work activities undertaken by yourself. Evidence from simulated activities is **only** acceptable for performance criterion d) in this element.

You must show evidence that you identify **both** of the following types of **development needs**

- to meet organisational objectives
- to meet individual aspirations.

You must also show evidence that you identify development needs for at least **four** of the following types of **personnel**

- internal
- external
- permanent
- temporary
- full-time
- part-time
- paid
- voluntary.

You must also show evidence that you seek guidance from at least **one** of the following types of **specialists**

- within your organisation
- from outside your organisation.

You must, however, convince your assessor that you have the necessary knowledge, understanding and skills to be able to perform competently in respect of **all** aspects of **personnel** and **specialists**, listed above.

**Develop teams and individuals
to enhance performance**

Element C10.2

Plan the development of teams and individuals

Performance criteria

You must ensure that

a) your plans reflect the identified training and development needs of all the **personnel** you are responsible for

b) your plans contain clear, relevant and realistic development objectives

c) your plans clearly identify the processes you will use and the resources you need

d) your plans are capable of being implemented within the defined timescales

e) where resources are insufficient to meet all identified needs, your plans accurately reflect organisational priorities

f) you present your plans to **relevant people** in an appropriate and timely manner

g) you update your plans at regular intervals after discussion and agreement with **relevant people**.

Knowledge requirements

You need to know and understand

Communication
- how to present your plans in a way which will positively influence the decision-making of relevant people.

Equal opportunities
- the importance of equality of opportunity in planning the development of team members.

Involvement and motivation
- the importance of agreeing development plans with those involved, and processes which may be used to achieve such agreement.

Organisational context
- the correct procedures for presenting plans for the development of teams and individuals.

Planning
- the importance of effective planning to human resource development
- the principles of good practice which underpin human resource development planning
- how to develop effective and realistic plans for individual and team development.

Training and development
- the team development needs which you have identified, and how your plans will help to meet these
- the importance of prioritising development activities and how to do this.

Evidence requirements

You must prove that you *plan the development of teams and individuals* to the National Standard of competence.

To do this, you must provide evidence to convince your assessor that you consistently meet **all** the performance criteria.

Your evidence must be the result of real work activities undertaken by yourself. Evidence from simulated activities is **only** acceptable for performance criterion e) in this element.

You must show evidence that your plans meet the development needs for at least **four** of the following types of **personnel**

- internal
- permanent
- full-time
- paid
- external
- temporary
- part-time
- voluntary.

You must also show evidence that you present your plans to at least **two** of the following types of **relevant people**
- team members
- colleagues working at the same level as yourself
- higher-level managers or sponsors
- specialists.

You must, however, convince your assessor that you have the necessary knowledge, understanding and skills to be able to perform competently in respect of **all** types of **personnel** and **relevant people**, listed above.

Develop teams and individuals
to enhance performance

Element C10.3

Develop teams to improve performance

Performance criteria

You must ensure that

a) the **development activities** which you organise support your team and organisational objectives

b) the **development activities** which you organise make best use of available resources

c) you provide all team members with equal access to relevant **development activities**

d) you demonstrate your own commitment to individual and team development through your personal support for, and involvement in, the **development activities**.

Knowledge requirements

You need to know and understand

Equal opportunities
- the importance of equality of opportunity in implementing development activities and how to ensure this.

Involvement and motivation
- how to motivate staff and win their commitment to, and participation in, development activities.

Leadership styles
- the importance of showing your own commitment to development activities
- how to present a positive role model in this regard to team members.

Training and development
- the range of activities which you may use to develop your team
- how to select and implement development activities which are appropriate to the team members, their development needs and work, the context in which you are operating and the available resources
- how to ensure that development activities meet agreed objectives and plans.

Evidence requirements

You must prove that you *develop teams to improve performance* to the National Standard of competence.

To do this, you must provide evidence to convince your assessor that you consistently meet **all** the performance criteria.

Your evidence must be the result of real work activities undertaken by yourself. Evidence from simulated activities is **not** acceptable for this element.

You must show evidence that you use at least **two** of the following types of **development activities**
- naturally occurring learning opportunities at work
- specifically designed learning opportunities at work
- formal training
- informal training.

You must, however, convince your assessor that you have the necessary knowledge, understanding and skills to be able to perform competently in respect of **all** types of **development activities**, listed above.

Develop teams and individuals
to enhance performance

Element C10.4

Support individual learning and development

Performance criteria

You must ensure that:

a) the **support** you provide is consistent with the **individuals'** needs, their objectives and preferred learning styles

b) the **support** you provide takes account of the **individuals'** work constraints and overall team objectives

c) you give all team members equal access to **support** relevant to their learning needs

d) you monitor the **individuals'** learning and development carefully so that you can modify **support** promptly, according to their needs

e) you encourage, collect and respond constructively to feedback from **individuals** on the quality of **support** you provide

f) you give feedback to **individuals** at points most likely to reinforce learning and development

g) the feedback you give is accurate, objective and helpful

h) you identify and remove any obstacles to learning effectively and with the agreement of the **individuals** involved.

Knowledge requirements

You need to know and understand

Equal opportunities

- the importance of equality of opportunity in implementing development activities and how to ensure this.

Monitoring and evaluation

- the importance of monitoring individual progress
- how to monitor and evaluate individual progress and make adjustments according to a range of factors which you identify
- the importance of gathering feedback on the quality of support you provide
- how to encourage and enable the individuals you support to provide useful feedback
- the importance of providing accurate, objective and constructive feedback to individuals on their progress
- how to provide feedback according to the individual and the circumstances.

Providing support

- the importance of managers supporting individual learning and development
- the types of support for individual learning and development which your team members may need
- the importance of ensuring that methods of support fit the individuals' needs, objectives and preferred learning styles
- how to choose methods of support which are appropriate to individuals' needs
- the range of obstacles to learning and development which individuals may encounter, how to identify these and strategies to use in response to them.

Evidence requirements

You must prove that you *support individual learning and development* to the National Standard of competence.

To do this, you must provide evidence to convince your assessor that you consistently meet **all** the performance criteria.

Your evidence must be the result of real work activities undertaken by yourself. Evidence from simulated activities is **only** acceptable for performance criterion h) in this element.

You must show evidence that you provide at least **two** of the following types of **support**

- mentoring
- coaching
- provision of learning opportunities at work.

You must also show evidence that you support at least **one** of the following types of **individuals**

- team members
- colleagues working at the same level as yourself
- people working in another team whom you have been asked to support
- people working temporarily in your organisation.

You must, however, convince your assessor that you have the necessary knowledge, understanding and skills to be able to perform competently in respect of **all** types of **support** and **individuals**, listed above.

Develop teams and individuals
to enhance performance

Element C10.5

Assess the development of teams and individuals

Performance criteria

You must ensure that

a) you agree the **purpose** of the **assessment** and your own role in it with relevant people

b) you give opportunities to team members to contribute to their own and their team's **assessments**

c) you give all team members equal access to **assessment** against development objectives

d) you carry out the **assessments** objectively against clear, agreed criteria

e) you base the **assessments** on sufficient, valid and reliable information

f) you provide information on the results of the **assessments** to authorised people only, in an appropriate format and to agreed deadlines.

Knowledge requirements

You need to know and understand

Equal opportunities
- the importance of equality of opportunity in providing opportunities for teams and individuals to contribute to their own assessments and how to ensure this.

Information handling
- how to collect and validate the information you need
- the importance of confidentiality when carrying out and reporting assessments.

Involvement and motivation
- the importance of agreeing the purpose of the assessments with relevant people
- the importance of team members contributing to the assessment of their own progress and how to encourage and enable them to do so.

Organisational context
- procedures for reporting the results of assessment.

Training and development
- the importance of assessing team members against development activities
- the team's development objectives
- the range of purposes which assessments have
- the principles of fair and objective assessment
- the methods which may be used to assess the development of team members
- the information required to assess team members' development.

Evidence requirements

You must prove that you *assess the development of teams and individuals* to the National Standard of competence.

To do this, you must provide evidence to convince your assessor that you consistently meet **all** the performance criteria.

Your evidence must be the result of real work activities undertaken by yourself. Evidence from simulated activities is **not** acceptable for this element.

You must show evidence that you carry out assessments with at least **two** of the following types of **purpose**
- to identify further development needs
- to evaluate the effectiveness of development processes
- to appraise performance
- to recognise knowledge, skills and competence at work.

You must also show evidence that you carry out at least **two** of the following types of **assessment**
- testing of knowledge and skills
- observing performance at work
- assessing the contributions of colleagues and team members
- taking part in appraisal discussions.

You must, however, convince your assessor that you have the necessary knowledge, understanding and skills to be able to perform competently in respect of **all** types of **purpose** and **assessment**, listed above.

Develop teams and individuals
to enhance performance

Element C10.6

Improve the development of teams and individuals

Performance criteria

You must ensure that

a) you give opportunities to those involved to help evaluate and improve **development activities**

b) your evaluation of the usefulness and applicability of **development activities** is based on sufficient valid and relevant information

c) your evaluation demonstrates the contribution **development activities** make to achieving team and organisational objectives

d) where **development activities** prove ineffective or inappropriate, you agree alternatives which are capable of meeting the development needs you have identified

e) you present your recommendations for improving overall development practice to **relevant people** in an appropriate and timely manner.

Knowledge requirements

You need to know and understand

Communication

- how to present recommendations in a way which is likely to influence decision-makers positively.

Continuous improvement

- the importance of continually reviewing and improving development activities to ongoing organisational effectiveness
- how to evaluate the contribution which development activities make to achieving team and organisational objectives and identify better alternatives
- the information which is needed to evaluate the usefulness and applicability of development activities.

Information handling

- how to collect and check the validity of the information you need.

Involvement and motivation

- the importance of giving opportunities to those involved to contribute to the evaluation and improvement of development activities
- how to encourage and enable those involved to provide useful feedback.

Organisational context

- procedures to follow when making recommendations to improve development activities.

Evidence requirements

You must prove that you *improve the development of teams and individuals* to the National Standard of competence.

To do this, you must provide evidence to convince your assessor that you consistently meet **all** the performance criteria.

Your evidence must be the result of real work activities undertaken by yourself. Evidence from simulated activities is **not** acceptable for this element.

You must show evidence that you evaluate and improve at least **two** of the following types of **development activities**

- naturally occurring learning opportunities at work
- specifically designed learning opportunities at work
- formal training
- informal training.

You must also show evidence that you pass on your recommendations to at least **two** of the following types of **relevant people**

- team members
- colleagues working at the same level as yourself
- higher-level managers or sponsors
- specialists.

You must, however, convince your assessor that you have the necessary knowledge, understanding and skills to be able to perform competently in respect of **all** types of **development activities** and **relevant people**, listed above.

Manage the performance of teams and individuals

Unit summary

This unit is about making the best use of your team and its members so that they can achieve your organisation's objectives. It covers allocating work, agreeing objectives, and setting out plans and methods of working. It also involves monitoring and evaluating the work of your team and its members and providing feedback to them on their performance.

This unit contains four elements

C13.1 *Allocate work to teams and individuals*
C13.2 *Agree objectives and work plans with teams and individuals*
C13.3 *Assess the performance of teams and individuals*
C13.4 *Provide feedback to teams and individuals on their performance.*

Personal competencies

In performing effectively in this unit, you will show that you

Acting assertively
- take a leading role in initiating action and making decisions
- take personal responsibility for making things happen
- take control of situations and events

Building teams
- actively build relationships with others
- make time available to support others
- encourage and stimulate others to make the best use of their abilities
- evaluate and enhance people's capability to do their jobs
- provide feedback designed to improve people's future performance
- show respect for the views and actions of others
- show sensitivity to the needs and feelings of others
- use power and authority in a fair and equitable manner
- keep others informed about plans and progress
- clearly identify what is required of others
- invite others to contribute to planning and organising work
- set objectives which are both achievable and challenging
- check individuals' commitment to a specific course of action
- use a variety of techniques to promote morale and productivity
- identify and resolve causes of conflict or resistance

Communicating
- listen actively, ask questions, clarify points and rephrase others' statements and check mutual understanding
- adopt communication styles appropriate to listeners and situations, including selecting an appropriate time and place
- confirm listeners' understanding through questioning and interpretation of non-verbal signals
- modify communication in response to feedback from listeners

Thinking and taking decisions
- break processes down into tasks and activities
- take decisions which are realistic for the situation.

Manage the performance of teams and individuals

Element C13.1

Allocate work to teams and individuals

Performance criteria

You must ensure that

a) you give opportunities to your team members to recommend how you should **allocate** work within the team

b) your **allocation** of work makes the best use of your team's resources and the abilities of all its members

c) your **allocation** of work provides your team members with suitable learning opportunities to meet their personal development objectives

d) your **allocation** of work is consistent with your team's objectives, and the objectives, policies and values of your organisation

e) you clearly define the responsibilities of your team and its individual members, and the limits of their authority

f) you provide sufficient **information** on your **allocation** of work in a manner and at a level and pace appropriate to the individuals concerned

g) you confirm team and individual understanding of, and commitment to, work **allocations** at appropriate intervals

h) where team resources are insufficient, you reach agreement with **relevant people** on the prioritisation of objectives or reallocation of resources

i) you inform your team and its members of changes to work **allocations** in a way which minimises the impact on time, cost and inconvenience.

Knowledge requirements

You need to know and understand

Communication
- the importance of defining and communicating team and individual responsibilities clearly
- how to communicate team and individual responsibilities clearly to those involved
- how to develop and present work plans using spoken, written and graphical means.

Delegation
- the importance of the effective allocation of work to your team's performance and your role and responsibilities in relation to this
- the factors which you need to consider when allocating work to individuals within the team
- how to match the allocation of work to learning needs and individual development plans
- how to prioritise and re-prioritise work allocations according to resource availability
- how your changes to work allocations and negotiations around them can impact on cost, time and convenience.

Involvement and motivation
- why your team members should have the opportunity to recommend work allocations
- how to encourage and enable team members to provide suggestions on the allocation of work and be committed to their responsibilities.

Organisational context
- your team objectives, and the organisational policies and values which have a bearing on the allocation of work within your team
- the relevant people with whom negotiations on the allocation of resources need to take place

Evidence requirements

You must prove that you *allocate work to teams and individuals* to the National Standard of competence.

To do this, you must provide evidence to convince your assessor that you consistently meet **all** the performance criteria.

Your evidence must be the result of real work activities undertaken by yourself. Evidence from simulated activities is **only** acceptable for performance criterion h) in this element.

You must show evidence that you make **allocations** covering **both** of the following contexts
- normal working
- emergencies.

You must show evidence that you provide at least **two** of the following types of **information**
- spoken
- written
- graphical.

You must also show evidence that you reach agreement with at least **two** of the following types of **relevant people**
- team members
- colleagues working at the same level as yourself
- higher-level managers or sponsors
- customers
- suppliers.

You must, however, convince your assessor that you have the necessary knowledge, understanding and skills to be able to perform competently in respect of **all** types of **information** and **relevant people**, listed above.

Manage the performance of
teams and individuals

Element C13.2

Agree objectives and work plans with teams and individuals

Performance criteria

You must ensure that

a) you give opportunities to your **team members** to help define their own **objectives and work plans**

b) you develop **objectives and work plans** which are consistent with team and organisational objectives and agree these with all personnel in your area of responsibility

c) the **objectives, work plans** and schedules are realistic and achievable within **organisational constraints**

d) the **objectives and work plans** take account of **team members'** abilities and development needs

e) you explain the **objectives and work plans** in sufficient detail and at a level and pace appropriate to your individual **team members**

f) you confirm team and individual understanding of, and commitment to, **objectives and work plans** at appropriate intervals

g) you provide advice and guidance on how to achieve **objectives** in sufficient detail and at times appropriate to the needs of teams and individuals

h) you update the **objectives and work plans** regularly and take account of any individual, team and organisational changes.

Knowledge requirements

You need to know and understand

Communication

- the importance of good communication when explaining objectives and work plans.

Involvement and motivation

- the importance of consulting with team members and achieving consensus and agreement on objectives and work plans
- how to encourage and enable team members to define their own work objectives and plans
- how to gain the commitment of team members to objectives and work plans
- the types of issues on which your team members may need advice and guidance.

Organisational context

- the organisational objectives and constraints which have a bearing on objectives and work plans.

Planning

- how to identify and devise objectives and work plans for the short, medium and long term
- the importance of agreeing objectives and work plans which are realistic and achievable
- how to match objectives and work plans with individuals' abilities and development needs
- the importance of regularly updating objectives and work plans
- the difference between someone who is within the manager's line management control and someone for whom the manager has functional responsibility, and the implications this difference may have for planning work.

Evidence requirements

You must prove that you *agree objectives and work plans with teams and individuals* to the National Standard of competence.

To do this, you must provide evidence to convince your assessor that you consistently meet **all** the performance criteria.

Your evidence must be the result of real work activities undertaken by yourself. Evidence from simulated activities is **not** acceptable for this element.

You must show evidence that you involve and plan work with at least **one** of the following types of **team member**

- people for whom you have line responsibility
- people for whom you have functional responsibility.

You must show evidence that you agree at least **two** of the following types of **objectives and work plans**

- short-term
- medium-term
- long-term.

You must also show evidence that you take account of **all** of the following types of **organisational constraints**

- organisational objectives
- organisational policies
- resources.

You must, however, convince your assessor that you have the necessary knowledge, understanding and skills to be able to perform competently in respect of **all** types of **team member** and **objectives and work plans**, listed above.

Manage the performance of
teams and individuals

Element C13.3

Assess the performance of teams and individuals

Performance criteria

You must ensure that

a) you clearly explain the **purpose** of **monitoring and assessment** to all those involved

b) you give opportunities to teams and individuals to **monitor and assess** their own performance against objectives and work plans

c) you **monitor** the performance of teams and individuals at times most likely to maintain and improve effective performance

d) your **assessment** of the performance of teams and individuals is based on sufficient, valid and reliable **information**

e) you carry out your **assessments** objectively, against clear, agreed criteria

f) your **assessments** take due account of the personal circumstances of team members and the **organisational constraints** on their work.

Knowledge requirements

You need to know and understand

Communication

- the importance of being clear yourself about the purpose of monitoring and assessment and communicating this effectively to those involved.

Continuous improvement

- the importance of monitoring and assessing the ongoing performance of teams and individuals
- different purposes of work monitoring and assessment
- how to make fair and objective assessments
- how to monitor and assess the performance of teams and individuals
- the standards against which work is to be assessed
- the information needed to assess the performance of teams and individuals.

Information handling

- how the necessary information should be gathered and validated.

Involvement and motivation

- the importance of providing opportunities to team members to monitor and assess their own work, and how to enable this.

Organisational context

- the organisational constraints which may affect the achievement of objectives.

Providing support

- the types of personal circumstances which may impact on individual performance.

Evidence requirements

You must prove that you *assess the performance of teams and individuals* to the National Standard of competence.

To do this, you must provide evidence to convince your assessor that you consistently meet **all** the performance criteria.

Your evidence must be the result of real work activities undertaken by yourself. Evidence from simulated activities is **not** acceptable for this element.

You must show evidence that your assessments have at least **two** of the following types of **purpose**

- assuring that objectives have been achieved
- assuring that quality and customer requirements have been met
- appraising team or individual performance
- assessing performance for reward
- recognising competent performance and achievement.

You must show evidence that you use at least **one** of the following types of **monitoring and assessment**

- specific to one activity or objective
- general to overall performance of the team or individual.

You must show evidence that you use **both** of the following types of **information**

- qualitative
- quantitative.

You must also show evidence that you take account of **all** the following types of **organisational constraints**

- organisational objectives
- organisational policies
- resources.

You must, however, convince your assessor that you have the necessary knowledge, understanding and skills to be able to perform competently in respect of **all** types of **purpose** and **monitoring and assessment**, listed above.

Manage the performance of
teams and individuals

Element C13.4

Provide feedback to teams and individuals on their performance

Performance criteria

You must ensure that

a) you provide **feedback** to teams and individuals in a **situation** and in a **form** and manner most likely to maintain and improve their performance

b) the **feedback** you provide is clear, and is based on your objective assessment of their performance against agreed objectives

c) your **feedback** acknowledges your team members' achievement

d) your **feedback** provides your team members with constructive suggestions and encouragement for improving future performance against their work and development objectives

e) the way in which you provide **feedback** shows respect for individuals and the need for confidentiality

f) you give opportunities to teams and individuals to respond to **feedback**, and to recommend how they could improve their performance in the future.

Knowledge requirements

You need to know and understand

Communication

- the importance of good communication skills when providing feedback
- how to provide both positive and negative feedback to team members on their performance
- how to choose an appropriate time and place to give feedback to teams and individuals
- how to provide feedback in a way which encourages your team members to feel that you respect them.

Continuous improvement

- the importance of providing clear and accurate feedback to your team members on their performance and your role and responsibilities in relation to this.

Information handling

- the principles of confidentiality when providing feedback – which people should receive which pieces of information.

Involvement and motivation

- how to motivate team members and gain their commitment by providing feedback
- the importance of being encouraging when providing feedback to team members and showing respect for those involved
- the importance of providing constructive suggestions on how performance can be improved
- the importance of giving those involved the opportunity to provide suggestions on how to improve their work.

Evidence requirements

You must prove that you *provide feedback to teams and individuals on their performance* to the National Standard of competence.

To do this, you must provide evidence to convince your assessor that you consistently meet **all** the performance criteria.

Your evidence must be the result of real work activities undertaken by yourself. Evidence from simulated activities is **not** acceptable for this element.

You must show evidence that you provide **both** of the following types of **feedback**
- positive
- negative.

You must show evidence that you use **both** of the following **forms** of feedback
- spoken
- written.

You must also show evidence that you give feedback in at least **three** of the following types of **situation**
- during normal day-to-day activities
- when required to maintain motivation, morale and effectiveness
- during formal appraisals
- at team meetings and briefings
- during confidential discussions of work.

You must, however, convince your assessor that you have the necessary knowledge, understanding and skills to be able to perform competently in respect of **all** types of **situation**, listed above.

Respond to poor performance in your team

Unit summary

This unit is about helping to deal with team members whose performance is unsatisfactory. It covers identifying their problems and providing help to deal with them. It also covers contributing to disciplinary and grievance procedures when work is consistently below standard or if a team member has a serious complaint against your organisation or someone in it.

This unit contains two elements

C15.1 *Help team members who have problems affecting their performance*
C15.2 *Contribute to implementing disciplinary and grievance procedures.*

Personal competencies

In performing effectively in this unit, you will show that you

Acting assertively
- act in an assured and unhesitating manner when faced with a challenge
- state your own position and views clearly in conflict situations
- maintain your beliefs, commitment and effort in spite of set-backs or opposition

Behaving ethically
- comply with legislation, industry regulation, professional and organisational codes
- show integrity and fairness in decision-making

Building teams
- make time available to support others
- encourage and stimulate others to make the best use of their abilities
- show respect for the views and actions of others
- show sensitivity to the needs and feelings of others
- use power and authority in a fair and equitable manner
- clearly identify what is required of others
- check individuals' commitment to a specific course of action
- use a variety of techniques to promote morale and productivity
- identify and resolve causes of conflict or resistance

Communicating
- listen actively, ask questions, clarify points and rephrase others' statements to check mutual understanding
- confirm listeners' understanding through questioning and interpretation of non-verbal signals
- encourage listeners to ask questions or rephrase statements to clarify their understanding
- modify communication in response to feedback from listeners

Focusing on results
- maintain a focus on objectives
- establish and communicate high expectations of performance, including setting an example to others
- monitor quality of work and progress against plans
- continually strive to identify and minimise barriers to excellence.

Respond to poor performance
in your team

Element C15.1

Help team members who have problems affecting their performance

Performance criteria

You must ensure that

a) you promptly identify poor performance and bring it directly to the attention of the **team member** concerned

b) you give the **team member** the opportunity to discuss actual or potential **problems** affecting their performance

c) you discuss these issues with the **team member** at a time and place appropriate to the type, seriousness and complexity of the **problem**

d) you gather and check as much information as possible to identify the nature of the **problem**

e) you agree with the **team member** a course of action which is appropriate, timely and effective

f) where necessary, you refer the **team member** to support services appropriate to their individual circumstances

g) the way you respond to **team members' problems** maintains respect for the individual and the need for confidentiality

h) you promptly inform relevant people of **problems** beyond your level of responsibility or competence.

Knowledge requirements

You need to know and understand

Communication

- the importance of providing opportunities for team members to discuss problems
- how to encourage and enable team members to talk frankly about their problems.

Information handling

- the importance of confidentiality.

Monitoring and evaluation

- the importance of promptly identifying poor performance and bringing it directly to team members' attention.

Providing support

- your role and responsibilities in dealing with team members' problems
- the types of problems which your team members may encounter at work
- how to identify problems which the individual is experiencing and devise appropriate responses
- the importance of agreeing a course of action with the team member involved
- how to decide when the problem goes beyond your own level of competence and responsibility
- the range of support services which exists inside and outside your organisation.

Working relationships

- the importance of maintaining respect for the individual
- the limits beyond which you should not go in becoming involved in the individual's problem.

Evidence requirements

You must prove that you *help team members who have problems affecting their performance* to the National Standard of competence.

To do this, you must provide evidence to convince your assessor that you consistently meet **all** the performance criteria.

Your evidence must be the result of real work activities undertaken by yourself. Evidence from simulated activities is **only** acceptable for performance criterion f) in this element.

You must show evidence that you help at least **one** of the following types of **team members**

- people for whom you have line management responsibility
- people for whom you have functional responsibility.

You must also show evidence that you help team members with at least **one** of the following types of **problems**

- arising from work-related factors
- arising from external personal factors.

You must, however, convince your assessor that you have the necessary knowledge, understanding and skills to be able to perform competently in respect of **all** types of **team members** and **problems**, listed above.

Respond to poor performance in your team

Contribute to implementing disciplinary and grievance procedures

Performance criteria

You must ensure that

a) your team members have clear, accurate and timely **information** regarding disciplinary and grievance procedures

b) your **contributions** to disciplinary and grievance procedures are provided in a fair, impartial and timely way

c) your **contributions** to implementing disciplinary and grievance procedures are consistent with your level of authority

d) your **contributions** to implementing disciplinary and grievance procedures maintain respect for the individual and the need for confidentiality.

Knowledge requirements

You need to know and understand

Disciplinary and grievance procedures

- the importance of effectively applying disciplinary and grievance procedures and your responsibilities in relation to this
- situations in which disciplinary and grievance procedures should be implemented
- the importance of informing team members about disciplinary and grievance procedures, appropriate times to do so and methods to use
- the importance of fairness, impartiality and responding in a timely way when dealing with disciplinary and grievance procedures.

Information handling

- the importance of confidentiality when dealing with disciplinary and grievance procedures – who may receive what information.

Legal requirements

- legal requirements relevant to disciplinary and grievance procedures.

Organisational context

- organisational requirements relevant to disciplinary and grievance procedures.

Working relationships

- the importance of maintaining respect for the individual when dealing with disciplinary and grievance procedures.

Evidence requirements

You must prove that you *contribute to implementing disciplinary and grievance procedures* to the National Standard of competence.

To do this, you must provide evidence to convince your assessor that you consistently meet **all** the performance criteria.

Your evidence should be the result of real work activities undertaken by yourself. However, evidence from simulated activities **is** acceptable for this element.

You must show evidence that you provide **both** of the following types of **information**
- organisational
- legal.

You must also show evidence that you make at least **one** of the following types of **contributions**
- requested by others
- on your own initiative.

You must, however, convince your assessor that you have the necessary knowledge, understanding and skills to be able to perform competently in respect of **both** types of **contributions**, listed above.

Facilitate meetings

Unit summary

This unit is about facilitating meetings so that objectives can be achieved. It covers leading meetings and making contributions to meetings.

This unit contains two elements

D2.1 *Lead meetings*
D2.2 *Make contributions to meetings.*

Personal competencies

In performing effectively in this unit, you will show that you

acting assertively

- take a leading role in initiating action and making decisions
- act in an assured and unhesitating manner when faced with a challenge
- say no to unreasonable requests

building teams

- actively build relationships with others
- show respect for the views and actions of others
- show sensitivity to the needs and feelings of others
- use power and authority in a fair and equitable manner
- invite others to contribute to planning and organising work

communicating

- listen actively, ask questions, clarify points and rephrase others' statements to check mutual understanding
- identify the information needs of listeners
- adopt communication styles appropriate to listeners and situations, including selecting an appropriate time and place
- confirm listeners' understanding through questioning and interpretation of non-verbal signals
- encourage listeners to ask questions or rephrase statements to clarify their understanding
- modify communication in response to feedback from listeners

focusing on results

- prioritise objectives and schedule work to make best use of time and resources

influencing others

- present yourself positively to others
- use a variety of means to influence others

searching for information

- actively encourage the free exchange of information
- push for concrete information in an ambiguous situation

thinking and making decisions

- produce a variety of solutions before taking a decision
- reconcile and make use of a variety of perspectives when making sense of a situation
- produce your own ideas from experience and practice
- take decisions which are realistic for the situation.

Facilitate meetings

Element D2.1

Lead meetings

Performance criteria

You must ensure that

a) you give people, appropriate to the context and **purpose** of the **meeting**, sufficient notice and information to allow them to contribute effectively

b) everyone attending the **meeting** agrees the objectives of the meeting at the start

c) you allocate discussion time to topics in a way which is consistent with their importance, urgency and complexity

d) your style of leadership helps those attending the **meeting** to make useful contributions

e) you discourage unhelpful arguments and digressions

f) you present information and provide summaries clearly, at appropriate points during the **meeting**

g) the **meeting** achieves its objectives within the allocated time

h) agreed decisions and recommendations fall within the group's authority

i) you give clear, accurate and concise information about decisions and recommendations to those who need it

j) you seek feedback from those attending and use this to improve the effectiveness of future **meetings**.

Knowledge requirements

You need to know and understand

Communication

- how to identify unhelpful arguments and digressions, and strategies which may be used to discourage these
- how to present information during meetings
- how to get and use feedback from others

Leadership styles

- styles of leadership which can be used to run meetings and how to choose a style according the nature of the meeting

Meetings

- the value and limitations of meetings as a method of exchanging information and making decisions
- how to determine when meetings are the most effective method of dealing with issues and possible alternatives which may be used
- potential differences between meetings which are internal and those involving people from outside
- the purpose of agendas and how to devise agendas according to the issues, intended outcomes and time available
- the importance of determining the purpose and objectives of meetings and how to do so
- the importance of summarising discussions and decisions during meetings and at what points this is appropriate
- how to manage discussions so that the objectives of the meeting are met within the allocated time
- the importance of ensuring decisions taken are within the authority of the meeting

Organisational context

- how to determine who are the necessary people to attend the meeting
- procedures to follow when calling meetings and preparing for them.

Evidence requirements

You must prove that you *lead meetings* to the National Standard of competence.

To do this, you must provide evidence to convince your assessor that you consistently meet **all** the performance criteria.

Your evidence must be the result of real work activities undertaken by yourself. Evidence from simulated activities is **not** acceptable for this element.

You must show evidence of leading meetings with **two** of the following **purposes**

- information giving
- consultation
- decision making.

You must also show evidence of leading **one** of the following types of **meeting**

- involving people from within your organisation
- involving people outside your organisation.

You must, however, convince your assessor that you have the necessary knowledge, understanding and skills to be able to perform competently in respect of **all** types of **purposes** and **meetings** listed above.

Facilitate meetings

Element D2.2

Make contributions to meetings

Performance criteria

You must ensure that

a) your preparation for the **meeting** is sufficient to enable you to participate effectively

b) you consult with the **people** you are representing sufficiently to allow them to present their views effectively

c) your contributions to the **meeting** are clear, concise and relevant

d) your contributions to the **meeting** help to clarify problems and identify and assess possible solutions

e) you acknowledge and discuss the contributions and viewpoints of others in a constructive manner

f) you give clear, accurate and concise information about decisions made at the **meeting** promptly to those who need it.

Knowledge requirements

You need to know and understand

Communication

- the information concerning the decisions and recommendations of the meeting which need to be conveyed to others and how to ensure that this has been done effectively

Meetings

- how to prepare for meetings according to different roles and responsibilities which you may have in relation to the meeting
- the importance of consulting in advance with those you are representing and how to do so
- the importance of making clear, concise and relevant contributions to meetings and how to ensure your contributions meet these criteria
- how to identify and analyse the problems discussed in meetings and make contributions capable of clarifying and resolving these

Working relationships

- the importance of constructively acknowledging the contributions and viewpoints of others and how to do so.

Evidence requirements

You must prove that you *make contributions to meetings* to the National Standard of competence.

To do this, you must provide evidence to convince your assessor that you consistently meet **all** the performance criteria.

Your evidence must be the result of real work activities undertaken by yourself. Evidence from simulated activities is **not** acceptable for this element.

You must also show evidence of contributing to **one** of the following types of **meetings**

- involving people from within your organisation
- involving people outside your organisation.

You must show evidence of representing **one** of the following types of **people**

- individuals
- groups.

You must, however, convince your assessor that you have the necessary knowledge, understanding and skills to be able to perform competently in respect of **all** types of **meetings** and **people** listed above.

Promote energy efficiency

Unit summary

This unit is about encouraging a culture of energy efficiency within the organisation and promoting the organisation's achievements in energy efficiency to outside audiences.

This unit contains two elements

E3.1   *Promote energy efficiency throughout the organisation*
E3.2   *Promote the organisation's achievements in energy efficiency.*

Personal competencies

In performing effectively in this unit, you will show that you

Acting strategically
- display an understanding of how the different parts of the organisation and its environment fit together
- clearly relate goals and actions to the strategic aims of the organisation
- take opportunities when they arise to achieve the longer-term aims or needs of your organisation

Communicating
- identify the information needs of listeners
- adopt communication styles appropriate to listeners and situations, including selecting an appropriate time and place
- use a variety of media and communication aids to reinforce points and maintain interest
- confirm listeners' understanding through questioning and interpretation of non-verbal signals
- modify communication in response to feedback from listeners

Influencing others
- present yourself positively to others
- create and prepare strategies for influencing others
- use a variety of means to influence others
- understand the culture of your organisation and act to work within it or influence it

Searching for information
- establish information networks to search for and gather relevant information
- make best use of existing sources of information
- seek information from multiple sources
- challenge the validity and reliability of sources of information.

Promote energy efficiency

Element E3.1

Promote energy efficiency throughout the organisation

Performance criteria

You must ensure that

a) you effectively communicate the **benefits** of energy efficiency to people throughout the organisation

b) you **promote** the organisation's achievements in energy efficiency throughout the organisation

c) you persuade **relevant people** to communicate their commitment to a culture of energy efficiency and energy conservation

d) there is a shared understanding of the role each part of the organisation must play in energy efficiency

e) you encourage individuals in the organisation to play an active role in the drive for energy efficiency.

Knowledge requirements

You need to know and understand

Communication

- the principles and processes of effective communication and how to apply them
- how to communicate the benefits of energy efficiency to relevant people in the organisation
- how to promote an understanding of, and enthusiasm for, energy efficiency

Energy efficiency

- the benefits of the efficient use of energy

Involvement and motivation

- how to gain people's commitment to energy efficiency

Organisational context

- the organisation's achievements in energy efficiency and how these came about
- people who could be influential in developing an energy efficient culture and how to gain their active support
- the structure of the organisation, the roles and responsibilities of teams and individuals within it.

Evidence requirements

You must prove that you *promote energy efficiency throughout the organisation* to the National Standard of competence.

To do this, you must provide evidence to convince your assessor that you consistently meet **all** the performance criteria.

Your evidence must be the result of real work activities undertaken by yourself. Evidence from simulated activities is **not** acceptable for this element.

You must show evidence that your advice is based on at least **two** of the following types of **benefits**

- costs
- quality
- productivity
- environment
- safety.

You must show evidence that you gain the commitment of at least **two** of the following types of **relevant people**

- colleagues working at the same level as yourself
- higher-level managers or sponsors
- technical specialists
- suppliers.

You must also show evidence that you **promote** energy efficiency using at least **two** of the following formats

- written
- graphic
- audio-visual
- electronic.

You must, however, convince your assessor that you have the necessary knowledge, understanding and skills to be able to perform competently in respect of **all** types of **benefits**, **relevant people** and **promotion** listed above.

Promote energy efficiency

Element E3.2

Promote the organisation's achievements in energy efficiency

Performance criteria

You must ensure that

a) you accurately evaluate opportunities to create and sustain awareness of energy efficiency outside the organisation

b) you seize opportunities which effectively **promote** awareness of energy efficiency, the organisation's achievements and policy

c) the information you provide on the organisation's achievements is up-to-date and consistent with the organisation's policy

d) the way you **promote** the organisation's energy policy and achievements emphasises how they contribute to its success

e) you encourage **appropriate people** to communicate their views and you reply to them effectively.

Knowledge requirements

You need to know and understand

Communication
- the range of opportunities available to create and sustain awareness of energy efficiency
- how to identify and evaluate opportunities to create and sustain awareness of energy efficiency outside the organisation
- how to emphasise the contribution which its energy policy and achievements make to the organisation's success
- the range of available presentational techniques and how to use them effectively
- how to encourage feedback and respond to it appropriately

Energy efficiency
- the principal techniques and technologies which support the efficient use of energy

Information handling
- how to check whether information is current

Organisational context
- the organisation's achievements in energy efficiency and how they came about
- the organisation's policies and procedures on the use of energy and on publicising its achievements.

Evidence requirements

You must prove that you *promote the organisation's achievements in energy efficiency* to the National Standard of competence.

To do this, you must provide evidence to convince your assessor that you consistently meet **all** the performance criteria.

Your evidence must be the result of real work activities undertaken by yourself. Evidence from simulated activities is **not** acceptable for this element.

You must show evidence that you **promote** the organisation's policy and achievements using at least **two** of the following formats
- written
- graphic
- audio-visual
- electronic.

You must also show evidence that you encourage feedback from at least **two** of the following types of **appropriate people**
- suppliers
- customers/service users
- special interest groups
- regulatory bodies
- the community.

You must, however, convince your assessor that you have the necessary knowledge, understanding and skills to be able to perform competently in respect of **all** types of **promotion** and **appropriate people** listed above.

Identify improvements to energy efficiency

Unit summary

This unit is about helping the organisation improve its energy efficiency. It covers both identifying opportunities for improvement and making appropriate recommendations.

This unit contains two elements

E5.1 *Identify opportunities to improve energy efficiency*

E5.2 *Recommend improvements to energy efficiency.*

Personal competencies

In performing effectively in this unit, you will show that you

Communicating
- listen actively, ask questions, clarify points and rephrase others' statements to check mutual understanding
- identify the information needs of listeners
- adopt communication styles appropriate to listeners and situations, including selecting an appropriate time and place

Influencing others
- develop and use contacts to trade information, and obtain support and resources
- present yourself positively to others
- create and prepare strategies for influencing others
- use a variety of means to influence others
- understand the culture of your organisation and act to work within it or influence it

Searching for information
- establish information networks to search for and gather relevant information
- make best use of existing sources of information
- seek information from multiple sources
- challenge the validity and reliability of sources of information

Thinking and taking decisions
- break processes down into tasks and activities
- identify a range of elements in and perspectives on a situation
- identify implications, consequences or causal relationships in a situation
- use your own experience and evidence from others to identify problems and understand situations
- identify patterns or meanings from events and data which are not obviously related
- reconcile and make use of a variety of perspectives when making sense of a situation
- produce your own ideas from experience and practice
- take decisions which are realistic for the situation.

Identify improvements to
energy efficiency

Element E5.1

Identify opportunities to improve energy efficiency

Performance criteria

You must ensure that

a) you consistently identify developments
   and advances in energy efficiency best
   practice which are relevant to the
   organisation

b) you regularly identify new markets,
   products, services and technological
   innovations which offer improvements
   in energy efficiency

c) you regularly review **resources**, systems
   and operational activities to identify
   opportunities for improved energy
   efficiency

d) you select and use **resources** which
   optimise the use of energy throughout
   the organisation

e) you identify **opportunities** for recycling
   energy used for operational activities

f) you identify **external programmes**
   which support the organisation's energy
   efficiency initiatives

g) you encourage individuals and teams to
   identify **opportunities** which improve
   energy efficiency and contribute to a
   sustainable environment.

Knowledge requirements

You need to know and understand

Communication

- the principles and processes of effective communication and how to apply them

Energy efficiency

- how to identify opportunities for improved energy efficiency
- the principal developments and advances in energy efficiency best practice
- how to select and use resources which optimise energy use
- the range of new markets, products, services and technological innovations relevant to energy efficiency
- the principal energy recycling opportunities
- the range of external programmes which may support energy efficiency initiatives
- the main sources of information on developments in energy efficiency technology and best practice and how to make use of them

Environmental management

- the principle of sustainable development and how to work towards it

Involvement and motivation

- how to encourage individuals and teams to identify energy efficiency improvements

Organisational context

- organisational activities, systems and resources and their impact on energy efficiency.

Evidence requirements

You must prove that you *identify opportunities to improve energy efficiency* to the National Standard of competence.

To do this, you must provide evidence to convince your assessor that you consistently meet **all** the performance criteria.

Your evidence must be the result of real work activities undertaken by yourself. Evidence from simulated activities is **not** acceptable for this element.

You must show evidence that you review at least **two** of the following types of **resources**

- money
- people
- premises
- equipment
- materials
- energy.

You must show evidence that you identify at least **two** of the following types of **opportunities**

- products
- services
- technological innovation
- design and modification of systems
- equipment and buildings
- recycling
- insulation.

You must also show evidence that you identify at least **two** of the following types of **external programmes**

- grant aid
- environmental measures
- local
- national and EU conservation initiatives
- Best Practice Programme.

You must, however, convince your assessor that you have the necessary knowledge, understanding and skills to be able to perform competently in respect of **all** types of **resources**, **opportunities** and **external programmes** listed above.

Identify improvements to
energy efficiency

Element E5.2

Recommend improvements to energy efficiency

Performance criteria

You must ensure that

a) you accurately evaluate the **advantages and disadvantages** to the organisation of possible energy efficiency improvements

b) you assess advances in technology for their applicability to the organisation's systems and activities

c) you accurately evaluate alternative energy sources and suppliers for cost savings and energy efficiency

d) you make recommendations based on your evaluations in line with organisational requirements

e) you seek further advice from appropriate people, where necessary.

Knowledge requirements

You need to know and understand

Analytical techniques

- how to assess the advantages and disadvantages of alternative courses of action
- how to assess the applicability of technological advances in the field of energy management

Communication

- the principles and processes of effective communication and how to apply them
- how to present advice to individuals and teams

Energy efficiency

- the range of energy efficiency improvements which can be made
- developments in energy efficiency technology and best practice
- the range of energy sources and their features and benefits
- the range of available and relevant suppliers, tariffs and fuel costs

Organisational context

- the operational systems and practices in the organisation
- the organisational requirements for providing advice and recommendations
- how to decide when further advice is necessary and who to go to.

Evidence requirements

You must prove that you *recommend improvements to energy efficiency* to the National Standard of competence.

To do this, you must provide evidence to convince your assessor that you consistently meet **all** the performance criteria.

Your evidence must be the result of real work activities undertaken by yourself. Evidence from simulated activities is acceptable **only** for performance criterion e) in this element.

You must show evidence that you evaluate at least **two** of the following types of **advantages and disadvantages**

- safety
- cost
- reliability
- environment
- quality.

You must, however, convince your assessor that you have the necessary knowledge, understanding and skills to be able to perform competently in respect of **all** types of **advantages and disadvantages** listed above.

Provide advice and support for the development of energy efficient practices

Unit summary

This unit is about helping the organisation develop energy efficient practices. It covers supporting the development of a culture of energy awareness and advising people in the organisation on energy efficient practices.

This unit contains two elements

E6.1 *Support the development of a culture of energy awareness*
E6.2 *Provide advice and support for energy efficient practices.*

Personal competencies

In performing effectively in this unit, you will show that you

Communicating
- listen actively, ask questions, clarify points and rephrase others' statements to check mutual understanding
- identify the information needs of listeners
- adopt communication styles appropriate to listeners and situations, including selecting an appropriate time and place
- use a variety of media and communication aids to reinforce points and maintain interest
- confirm listeners' understanding through questioning and interpretation of non-verbal signals

Influencing others
- develop and use contacts to trade information, and obtain support and resources
- present yourself positively to others
- create and prepare strategies for influencing others
- use a variety of means to influence others
- understand the culture of your organisation and act to work within it or influence it

Searching for information
- establish information networks to search for and gather relevant information
- make best use of existing sources of information
- seek information from multiple sources

Thinking and taking decisions
- identify implications, consequences or causal relationships in a situation
- use your own experience and evidence from others to identify problems and understand situations
- identify patterns or meaning from events and data which are not obviously related
- reconcile and make use of a variety of perspectives when making sense of a situation
- produce your own ideas from experience and practice
- take decisions which are realistic for the situation.

Provide advice and support for
the development of energy
efficient practices

Element E6.1

Support the development of a culture of energy awareness

Performance criteria

You must ensure that

a) you accurately identify the level of
energy awareness within the
organisation

b) you accurately identify effective ways of
increasing energy awareness within the
organisation

c) you develop, agree and implement an
effective programme of **activities** to
promote energy awareness

d) you develop efficient systems for
monitoring energy awareness and agree
these with **appropriate people**

e) you implement procedures to gather
and collate data from monitoring
systems

f) you report progress on the level of
energy awareness regularly, with
recommendations for further
improvements.

Knowledge requirements

You need to know and understand

Communication
- the principles and processes of effective communication and how to apply them
- how to consult and collaborate with appropriate people and agree the implementation of a programme of activities

Energy efficiency
- how to measure the level of energy awareness
- the range of methods and activities which may be used to increase energy awareness within an organisation and how to assess what methods would be most effective
- types of systems for monitoring energy awareness and how to develop these

Information handling
- how to develop and implement procedures to gather and collate data from monitoring systems
- how to decide the appropriate format and frequency for reporting progress on energy awareness levels
- how to use information to identify and recommend improvements
- sources of information on energy efficiency

Organisational context
- the structure and responsibilities within the organisation and how its activities interrelate.

Evidence requirements

You must prove that you *support the development of a culture of energy awareness* to the National Standard of competence.

To do this, you must provide evidence to convince your assessor that you consistently meet **all** the performance criteria.

Your evidence must be the result of real work activities undertaken by yourself. Evidence from simulated activities is **not** acceptable for this element.

You must show evidence that you use at least **two** of the following types of **activities** for promoting energy awareness
- publicity
- training
- motivation
- instruction.

You must also show evidence that you agree your promotional programme with, and report progress to, at least **two** of the following types of **appropriate people**

- higher-level managers or sponsors
- colleagues working at the same level as yourself
- technical specialists.

You must, however, convince your assessor that you have the necessary knowledge, understanding and skills to be able to perform competently in respect of **all** types of **activities** and **appropriate people** listed above.

Provide advice and support for the development of energy efficient practices

Element E6.2

Provide advice and support for energy efficient practices

Performance criteria

You must ensure that

a) you provide **relevant people** with accurate and up-to-date information on the impact of working practices on energy performance

b) you consistently encourage **relevant people** to evaluate working practices and improve energy performance

c) you identify the **effects** of energy performance on safety and the environment and communicate these to **relevant people**

d) you develop efficient systems to monitor energy performance which are suitable for the activities of the organisation

e) changes in working practices are monitored and accurately recorded in order to evaluate their **effects** on energy performance.

Knowledge requirements

You need to know and understand

Communication
- how to provide accurate and up-to-date information to teams and individuals

Energy efficiency
- the ways in which working practices may impact on energy performance
- the ways in which energy performance may impact on safety and the environment
- types of systems for monitoring energy performance and how to assess their suitability for the organisation's activities

Involvement and motivation
- how to encourage people to play an active role in energy efficiency

Legal requirements
- the main requirements of relevant health and safety legislation
- the main requirements of relevant environmental legislation

Monitoring and evaluation
- how to monitor and record changes in working practices

Organisational context
- the structure and responsibilities within the organisation and how its activities interrelate
- the importance of monitoring energy performance
- the activities and needs of the organisation.

Evidence requirements

You must prove that you *provide advice and support for energy efficient practices* to the National Standard of competence.

To do this, you must provide evidence to convince your assessor that you consistently meet **all** the performance criteria.

Your evidence must be the result of real work activities undertaken by yourself. Evidence from simulated activities is **not** acceptable for this element.

You must show evidence that you advise at least **two** of the following types of **relevant people**
- higher-level managers or sponsors
- colleagues working at the same level as yourself
- staff.

You must also show evidence that you identify and evaluate **both** of the following types of **effects**
- advantages
- disadvantages.

You must, however, convince your assessor that you have the necessary knowledge, understanding and skills to be able to perform competently in respect of **all** types of **relevant people** listed above.

Provide advice and support for improving energy efficiency

Unit summary

This unit is about helping teams and individuals to become more efficient in the ways they use energy. It covers getting them involved in energy efficiency activities, helping them to identify the knowledge and skills they need and helping them to develop this knowledge and these skills.

This unit contains three elements

E8.1 *Encourage involvement in energy efficiency activities*
E8.2 *Provide advice on the competences needed to use energy efficiently*
E8.3 *Provide advice on the training needed to use energy efficiently.*

Personal competencies

In performing effectively in this unit, you will show that you

Communicating

- identify the information needs of listeners
- adopt communication styles appropriate to listeners and situations, including selecting an appropriate time and place
- use a variety of media and communication aids to reinforce points and maintain interest
- present difficult ideas and problems in a way that promotes understanding
- confirm listeners' understanding through questioning and interpretation of non-verbal signals
- encourage listeners to ask questions or rephrase statements to clarify their understanding
- modify communication in response to feedback from listeners

Influencing others

- present yourself positively to others
- create and prepare strategies for influencing others
- use a variety of means to influence others

Searching for information

- make best use of existing sources of information
- seek information from multiple sources
- challenge the validity and reliability of sources of information

Thinking and making decisions

- identify a range of elements in and perspectives on a situation
- identify implications, consequences or causal relationships in a situation
- use your own experience and evidence from others to identify problems and understand situations
- identify patterns or meanings from events and data which are not obviously related
- build a total and valid picture from restricted or incomplete data.

UNIT E8

Provide advice and support for improving energy efficiency

Element E8.1

Encourage involvement in energy efficiency activities

Performance criteria

You must ensure that

a) you provide clear, relevant, sufficient and accessible information about energy efficient initiatives

b) you advise and encourage **relevant people** to help define their roles and responsibilities with regard to energy efficiency

c) you consistently enable **relevant people** to offer suggestions, ideas and views and to take an active part in improving the way the organisation manages energy

d) where it is not possible to act on a suggestion, you promptly provide clear and relevant reasons to those concerned

e) you consistently and effectively promote examples of good practice in energy efficiency within the organisation.

Knowledge requirements

You need to know and understand

Communication

- the principles and processes of effective communication and how to apply them
- the importance of giving clear feedback where suggestions are not taken up, and how to do this in a way which maintains morale

Energy efficiency

- the range of energy efficiency initiatives which may be used within the organisation
- a range of examples of good practice in energy efficiency and how to promote these within the organisation

Involvement and motivation

- the importance of getting people to take ownership of a problem and how to get them to do this
- how to enable people to come forward with suggestions, ideas and views
- how to enable people to take an active part in improving the way the organisation manages energy

Organisational context

- the structures and responsibilities within the organisation.

Evidence requirements

You must prove that you *encourage involvement in energy efficiency activities* to the National Standard of competence.

To do this, you must provide evidence to convince your assessor that you consistently meet **all** the performance criteria.

Your evidence must be the result of real work activities undertaken by yourself. Evidence from simulated activities is **not** acceptable for this element.

You must show evidence that your work in this area includes at least **two** of the following types of **relevant people**

- higher-level managers or sponsors
- colleagues working at the same level as yourself
- staff.

You must, however, convince your assessor that you have the necessary knowledge, understanding and skills to be able to perform competently in respect of **all** types of **relevant people** listed above.

Provide advice and support for
improving energy efficiency

Element E8.2

Provide advice on the competences needed to use energy efficiently

Performance criteria

You must ensure that

a) your **advice** takes account of all the knowledge and skills needed to achieve the organisation's energy plans

b) your **advice** takes full account of **resource** limitations

c) your **advice** is consistent with the organisation's policy and plans for energy usage

d) you provide **advice** in a manner and at a pace which meets the needs of those concerned

e) you give **relevant people** the opportunity to seek clarification of any areas of concern.

Knowledge requirements

You need to know and understand

Communication

- the principles and processes of effective communications and how to apply them
- the importance of providing people with the opportunity to ask questions and seek clarification and how to do this
- how to provide effective advice to relevant people in the organisation

Energy efficiency

- the range of knowledge and skills required to achieve energy management plans

Organisational context

- the organisation's energy policy, its strategy and plans for implementing this policy
- the organisation's resource limitations.

Evidence requirements

You must prove that you *provide advice on the competences needed to use energy efficiently* to the National Standard of competence.

To do this, you must provide evidence to convince your assessor that you consistently meet **all** the performance criteria.

Your evidence must be the result of real work activities undertaken by yourself. Evidence from simulated activities is **not** acceptable for this element.

You must show evidence that you take account of at least **two** of the following types of **resources**

- money
- people
- equipment
- energy
- premises
- materials.

You must show evidence that you provide **both** of the following types of **advice**

- written
- spoken.

You must also show evidence that your work in this area includes at least **two** of the following types of **relevant people**

- higher-level managers or sponsors
- colleagues working at the same level as yourself
- staff.

You must, however, convince your assessor that you have the necessary knowledge, understanding and skills to be able to perform competently in respect of **all** types of **resources** and **relevant people** listed above.

Provide advice and support for improving energy efficiency

Element E8.3

Provide advice on the training needed to use energy efficiently

Performance criteria

You must ensure that

a) you give **relevant people** effective opportunities to identify the knowledge and skills they need to use energy efficiently

b) you help **relevant people** identify suitable opportunities to develop their knowledge and skills in the efficient use of energy

c) the **advice** you give is sufficient to be able to plan appropriate **training and development activities**

d) you enable **relevant people** to give useful feedback on **training and development activities** and to recommend how these activities can be improved

e) where **training and development activities** prove to be unsuitable or ineffective, you recommend suitable alternatives for the future.

Knowledge requirements

You need to know and understand

Communication
- the principles and processes of effective communication and how to apply them

Energy efficiency
- the range of knowledge and skills required to use energy efficiently
- the range of opportunities available for developing knowledge and skills in energy efficiency

Training and development
- how to identify the knowledge and skills individuals require
- how to plan training and development activities
- how to encourage people to give feedback on the training and development they have received
- how to assess whether training and development has been suitable and effective or not.

Evidence requirements

You must prove that you *provide advice on the training needed to use energy efficiently* to the National Standard of competence.

To do this, you must provide evidence to convince your assessor that you consistently meet **all** the performance criteria.

Your evidence must be the result of real work activities undertaken by yourself. Evidence from simulated activities is acceptable **only** for performance criterion e) in this element.

You must show evidence that your work in this area includes at least **two** of the following types of **relevant people**
- higher-level managers or sponsors
- colleagues working at the same level as yourself
- staff.

You must show evidence that you provide **both** of the following types of **advice**
- written
- spoken.

You must also show evidence that you use **two** of the following types of **training and development activities**
- specially allocated work activities
- formal training
- informal development activities.

You must, however, convince your assessor that you have the necessary knowledge, understanding and skills to be able to perform competently in respect of **all** types of **relevant people** and **training and development activities** listed above.

Provide advice and support for the development and implementation of quality policies

Unit summary

This unit is about helping organisations to define quality policies and develop strategies to implement these policies throughout the organisation and its customer and supplier networks.

This unit contains two elements

F2.1 *Provide advice and support for the development of quality policies*
F2.2 *Provide advice and support for the development of strategies to implement quality policies.*

Personal competencies

In performing effectively in this unit, you will show that you

Acting strategically
- understand how the different parts of the organisation and its environment fit together
- work towards a clearly defined vision of the future
- clearly relate your goals and actions to the strategic aims of your organisation

Communicating
- adopt communication styles appropriate to listeners and situations, including selecting an appropriate time and place
- use a variety of media and communication aids to reinforce points and maintain interest
- present difficult ideas and problems in ways that promote understanding
- confirm listeners' understanding through questioning and interpretation of non-verbal signals

Influencing others
- present yourself positively to others
- create and prepare strategies for influencing others
- use a variety of means to influence others

Thinking and taking decisions
- break processes down into tasks and activities
- identify a range of elements in and perspectives on a situation
- identify implications, consequences or causal relationships in a situation
- use a range of ideas to explain the actions, needs and motives of others
- use your own experience and evidence from others to identify problems and understand situations
- build a total and valid picture from restricted or incomplete data
- produce a variety of solutions before taking a decision
- produce your own ideas from experience and practice
- take decisions which are realistic for the situation.

UNIT F2

Provide advice and support for the development and implementation of quality policies

Element F2.1

Provide advice and support for the development of quality policies

Performance criteria

You must ensure that

a) you explain the nature and purpose of quality concepts, standards, systems and programmes clearly and accurately to **relevant people**

b) you clearly explain the importance of performance measurement to the organisation's success

c) you clearly explain why a documented system for the implementation of quality is necessary and what benefits it is likely to bring

d) you encourage **relevant people** to articulate their vision of quality, and make their commitment to quality explicit, so that they can develop **policies** to support the organisation's mission

e) you highlight any inconsistencies in the aims and commitments of management and propose options for resolving them

f) any conflict between the aims of suppliers and customers and the organisation's vision of quality are resolved

g) you provide advice to management on appropriate methods of communicating quality **policies**.

Knowledge requirements

You need to know and understand

Communication
- the principles and processes of effective communication and how to apply them
- how to communicate quality policies.

Involvement and motivation
- how to help people commit themselves to quality and make this commitment explicit.

Organisational context
- key decision-makers and their preferred format for the presentation of information
- the organisation's vision, mission, objectives and strategies, values and policies
- the organisation's suppliers and customers, and their aims.

Quality management
- the range of quality concepts, standards, systems and programmes
- the principal performance measurement systems and their importance to the organisation's success
- the range of documented systems for quality assurance and the benefits they are likely to bring.

Strategic planning
- how to help people clarify their vision of quality.

Working relationships
- how to identify and resolve inconsistencies and conflicts.

Evidence requirements

You must prove that you *provide advice and support for the development of quality policies* to the National Standard of competence.

To do this, you must provide evidence to convince your assessor that you consistently meet **all** the performance criteria.

Your evidence must be the result of real work activities undertaken by yourself. Evidence from simulated activities is acceptable **only** for performance criteria e) and f) in this element.

You must show evidence that your work in this area involves at least **two** of the following types of **relevant people**
- higher-level managers or sponsors
- colleagues working at the same level as yourself
- team members
- customers
- suppliers.

You must also show evidence that you help develop **policies** relating to at least **three** of the following
- design of processes for producing goods
- design of processes for delivering services
- processes and systems within the organisation including documentation
- employees, including their training and development
- customers
- suppliers and procurement strategies.

You must, however, convince your assessor that you have the necessary knowledge, understanding and skills to be able to perform competently in respect of **all** types of **relevant people** and **policies**, listed above.

Provide advice and support for the development and implementation of quality policies

Element F2.2

Provide advice and support for the development of strategies to implement quality policies

Performance criteria

You must ensure that

a) you give **relevant people** the necessary information, opportunities and support to identify and select strategies which are consistent with the organisation's vision of quality

b) you accurately evaluate alternative strategies for implementing quality and identify their advantages, disadvantages and resource implications

c) you present the results of your evaluation to **relevant people** in an effective manner

d) you clarify and emphasise the role of suppliers in implementing policy and identify appropriate strategies to develop the organisation's supplier base

e) you give **relevant people** effective opportunities, information and support to translate customer needs into deliverable products and services at optimum cost and speed

f) you give **relevant people** the necessary information and support to design systems which control the delivery of products and services which are consistent with quality strategies and policies

g) you regularly monitor the implementation of quality policies against agreed criteria

h) you make recommendations to **relevant people** how they could improve quality policies and the way they are implemented.

Knowledge requirements

You need to know and understand

Analytical techniques
- how to evaluate alternative strategies for implementing quality policies.

Communication
- the principles and processes of effective communication and how to apply them
- how to make recommendations for improvements.

Customer relations
- how to identify customer needs and translate them into deliverable products and services.

Monitoring and evaluation
- how to develop and agree criteria to monitor the implementation of quality policies
- how to monitor the implementation of quality policies.

Organisational context
- the organisation's vision of quality
- the people within the organisation and its networks who need to be involved in implementing quality policies
- the organisation's structure and the responsibilities of people within it
- the organisation's current and potential customers and suppliers
- the organisation's capability for delivering products and services.

Quality management
- the role of suppliers in implementing quality policies
- the range of systems for controlling processes.

Strategic planning
- the range of strategies which may be adopted to implement quality policies.

Evidence requirements

You must prove that you *provide advice and support for the development of strategies to implement quality policies* to the National Standard of competence.

To do this, you must provide evidence to convince your assessor that you consistently meet **all** the performance criteria.

Your evidence must be the result of real work activities undertaken by yourself. Evidence from simulated activities is **not** acceptable for this element.

You must show evidence that you give support to at least **two** of the following types of **relevant people**
- higher-level managers or sponsors
- colleagues working at the same level as yourself
- team members
- customers
- suppliers.

You must, however, convince your assessor that you have the necessary knowledge, understanding and skills to be able to perform competently in respect of **all** types of **relevant people**, listed above.

Implement quality assurance systems

Unit summary

This unit is about ensuring that your organisation's products and services continuously meet the standard required by your customers. It covers setting up quality assurance systems, assuring quality by making sure these systems operate effectively and making recommendations for improvements to quality assurance systems.

This unit contains three elements

F4.1 *Establish quality assurance systems*
F4.2 *Maintain quality assurance systems*
F4.3 *Recommend improvements to quality assurance systems.*

Personal competencies

In performing effectively in this unit, you will show that you

Communicating
- listen actively, ask questions, clarify points and rephrase others' statements to check mutual understanding
- adopt communication styles appropriate to listeners and situations, including selecting an appropriate time and place
- encourage listeners to ask questions or rephrase statements to clarify their understanding

Focusing on results
- actively seek to do things better
- use change as an opportunity for improvement
- establish and communicate high expectations of performance, including setting an example to others
- monitor quality of work and progress against plans

Influencing others
- present yourself positively to others
- create and prepare strategies for influencing others
- use a variety of means to influence others
- understand the culture of the organisation and act to work within it or influence it

Thinking and taking decisions
- break processes down into tasks and activities
- use your own experience and evidence from others to identify problems and understand situations
- identify patterns or meaning from events and data which are not obviously related
- produce a variety of solutions before taking a decision
- produce your own ideas from experience and practice
- take decisions which are realistic for the situation.

Implement quality assurance systems

Element F4.1

Establish quality assurance systems

Performance criteria

You must ensure that

a) your analysis of processes is sufficient to determine appropriate **quality assurance systems** and measurements

b) you present your recommendations and rationale for establishing **quality assurance systems** to **relevant people** with the appropriate level of detail and degree of urgency

c) you agree implementation plans, taking account of feedback from **relevant people**

d) you provide opportunities for those involved in **quality assurance systems** to contribute to their development

e) the systems you set up clearly specify the processes, procedures and measurements required to ensure products and services are within the limits of acceptable quality

f) your **quality assurance systems** are capable of making sure that agreed customer requirements are consistently met

g) you **communicate** the establishment of **quality assurance systems** in a way which is clear, detailed and allows adequate time for preparation

h) you **communicate** the results and benefits of assuring quality at times most likely to gain the commitment of **relevant people** to the systems.

Knowledge requirements

You need to know and understand

Communication

- how to communicate effectively to colleagues, team members and higher-level managers and sponsors on quality assurance issues.

Customer relations

- the importance of customer focus in managing quality.

Involvement and motivation

- how to develop and present an effective case for the introduction of quality assurance systems
- the importance of consulting on the introduction of quality assurance systems and how to do so effectively
- how to gain the commitment of staff for quality assurance systems.

Quality management

- the importance of quality assurance and your role and responsibility in relation to this
- the meaning of quality in the context of managing activities
- the principles underpinning effective quality assurance systems and how to apply them
- the range of quality assurance systems available and their relative advantages and disadvantages to the activities for which you are responsible
- how to analyse work processes and determine the most appropriate quality assurance systems and measurements
- how to specify the requirements of a quality assurance system.

Evidence requirements

You must prove that you *establish quality assurance systems* to the National Standard of competence.

To do this, you must provide evidence to convince your assessor that you consistently meet **all** the performance criteria.

Your evidence must be the result of real work activities undertaken by yourself. Evidence from simulated activities is **not** acceptable for this element.

You must show evidence that you have established at least **one** of the following types of **quality assurance systems**
- externally validated
- devised and validated in-house.

You must show evidence of your work in this area with at least **three** of the following types of **relevant people**
- team members
- colleagues working at the same level as you
- higher-level managers or sponsors
- specialists.

You must also show evidence that your **communications** are in at least **two** of the following forms
- spoken
- written
- images.

You must, however, convince your assessor that you have the necessary knowledge, understanding and skills to be able to perform competently in respect of **all** types of **quality assurance systems, relevant people** and **communications**, listed above.

Implement quality assurance systems

Element F4.2

Maintain quality assurance systems

Performance criteria

You must ensure that

a) you present information on **quality assurance systems**, procedures and responsibilities to **relevant people** at a time and place and in a format appropriate to their needs

b) you confirm **relevant people's** understanding of, and commitment to, **quality assurance systems** at appropriate intervals

c) you collect and **evaluate** information, and report the results at required intervals, using agreed methods and against specified performance measures

d) you take prompt and effective action to clarify inadequate, contradictory or ambiguous information

e) you actively encourage **relevant people** freely to report actual and potential variations in quality

f) you take timely and effective action, consistent with quality assurance procedures, to rectify unacceptable variations in products and services.

Knowledge requirements

You need to know and understand

Communication
- how to communicate effectively with team members, colleagues and higher-level managers and sponsors on quality assurance issues.

Information handling
- how to validate information which may be inadequate, contradictory and ambiguous.

Involvement and motivation
- how to maintain staff commitment to quality assurance systems
- how to encourage and enable feedback on quality.

Quality management
- the importance of maintaining quality assurance systems and the procedures required to do so.

Evidence requirements

You must prove that you *maintain quality assurance systems* to the National Standard of competence.

To do this, you must provide evidence to convince your assessor that you consistently meet **all** the performance criteria.

Your evidence must be the result of real work activities undertaken by yourself. Evidence from simulated activities is acceptable **only** for performance criteria d) and f) in this element.

You must show evidence that you maintain **one** of the following types of **quality assurance systems**
- externally validated
- devised and validated in-house.

You must also show evidence of your work in this area with at least **three** of the following types of **relevant people**
- team members
- colleagues working at the same level as you
- higher-level managers or sponsors
- specialists.

You must also show evidence that you use **both** the following types of **evaluation** methods
- qualitative
- quantitative.

You must, however, convince your assessor that you have the necessary knowledge, understanding and skills to be able to perform competently in respect of **all** types of **quality assurance systems**, and **relevant people**, listed above.

Implement quality assurance
systems

Element F4.3

Recommend improvements to quality assurance systems

Performance criteria

You must ensure that

a) you provide opportunities for **relevant people** to suggest improvements to **quality assurance systems**

b) you base your **recommendations** on sufficient, valid and reliable information on the effectiveness and efficiency of **quality assurance systems**

c) your **recommendations** have the potential to improve the contribution which **quality assurance systems** make to the organisation and its customers

d) you present your **recommendations** to **relevant people** clearly, logically and in time to be of use

e) where **recommendations** are not accepted, you establish the reasons and present these to **relevant people** in a manner which maintains morale and motivation.

Knowledge requirements

You need to know and understand

Communication
- how to communicate effectively with team members, colleagues and higher-level managers and sponsors on quality assurance issues
- how to develop and argue an effective case for change.

Continuous improvement
- the importance of continuous improvement to the effectiveness of the team and organisation and your role and responsibilities in relation to this.

Customer relations
- the importance of customer focus in managing activities.

Involvement and motivation
- how to encourage and enable feedback on quality systems.

Information handling
- how to collect and validate sufficient information on the effectiveness of quality assurance systems to make recommendations on improvement.

Working relationships
- how to resolve disagreements and disputes in ways which maintain morale and motivation.

Evidence requirements

You must prove that you *recommend improvements to quality assurance systems* to the National Standard of competence.

To do this, you must provide evidence to convince your assessor that you consistently meet **all** the performance criteria.

Your evidence must be the result of real work activities undertaken by yourself. Evidence from simulated activities is acceptable **only** for performance criterion e) in this element.

You must show evidence that you have recommended improvements for at least **one** of the following types of **quality assurance systems**
- externally validated
- devised and validated in-house.

You must also show evidence that you work with at least **three** of the following types of **relevant people**
- team members
- colleagues working at the same level as you
- higher-level managers or sponsors
- specialists.

You must also show evidence that you make **both** of the following types of **recommendations**
- in response to request
- on own initiative.

You must, however, convince your assessor that you have the necessary knowledge, understanding and skills to be able to perform competently in respect of **all** types of **quality assurance systems**, and **relevant people**, listed above.

Monitor compliance with quality systems

Unit summary

This unit is about ensuring that all the processes of the organisation comply with quality systems. It covers planning to audit quality systems, implementing this plan and providing a report on the organisation's overall compliance with its quality systems.

This unit contains three elements

F6.1 *Plan to audit compliance with quality systems*
F6.2 *Implement the audit plan*
F6.3 *Report on compliance with quality systems.*

Personal competencies

In performing effectively in this unit, you will show that you

Building teams
- make time available to support others
- encourage and stimulate others to make the best use of their abilities
- evaluate and enhance people's capability to do their jobs
- provide feedback designed to improve people's future performance
- show respect for the views and actions of others
- show sensitivity to the needs and feelings of others
- use power and authority in a fair and equitable manner

Communicating
- listen actively, ask questions, clarify points and rephrase others' statements to check mutual understanding
- identify the information needs of listeners
- adopt communication styles appropriate to listeners and situations, including selecting an appropriate time and place

Focusing on results
- maintain a focus on objectives
- tackle problems and take advantage of opportunities as they arise
- prioritise objectives and schedule work to make best use of time and resources

Searching for information
- seek information from multiple sources
- challenge the validity and reliability of sources of information

Thinking and taking decisions
- break processes down into tasks and activities
- use your own experience and evidence from others to identify problems and understand situations
- identify patterns or meaning from events and data which are not obviously related
- build a total and valid picture from restricted or incomplete data
- take decisions which are realistic for the situation.

Monitor compliance with quality systems

Element F6.1

Plan to audit compliance with quality systems

Performance criteria

You must ensure that

a) you agree the scope and objectives of the **audits** with **relevant people**

b) you accurately identify processes in the organisation where non-compliance is most likely

c) you accurately identify the relative risks to the organisation of non-compliance with quality systems in each of the organisation's processes

d) you agree with **relevant people** a programme of **audits** which prioritises areas of greatest risk and likely non-compliance

e) you develop a sufficient number of competent people to carry out the programme of **audits**

f) your programme of **audits** complies with the organisation's quality policies and procedures.

Knowledge requirements

You need to know and understand

Analytical techniques
- how to assess the relative risks of non-compliance with quality systems.

Communication
- the principles and processes of effective communication and how to apply them.

Organisational context
- the relevant structures, responsibilities and processes within the organisation
- the people within the organisation with whom you must agree the scope, objectives and programme of audits
- the organisation's quality policy and procedures.

Quality management
- the principles of quality auditing and how to conduct an audit investigation
- how to agree the scope and objectives of quality audits
- how to assess which of the organisation's processes are likely not to comply with quality systems
- the knowledge and skills required by those who will carry out the audits, and how to assess and develop these skills and knowledge.

Evidence requirements

You must prove that you *plan to audit compliance with quality systems* to the National Standard of competence.

To do this, you must provide evidence to convince your assessor that you consistently meet **all** the performance criteria.

Your evidence must be the result of real work activities undertaken by yourself. Evidence from simulated activities is **not** acceptable for this element.

You must show evidence that you plan **one** of the following types of **audits**
- within your organisation
- in other organisations.

You must also show evidence that you agree the scope, objectives and programme of the audits with **one** of the following types of **relevant people**
- higher-level managers or sponsors
- colleagues working at the same level as yourself
- quality specialists.

You must, however, convince your assessor that you have the necessary knowledge, understanding and skills to be able to perform competently in respect of **all** types of **audits** and **relevant people**, listed above.

Monitor compliance with
quality systems

Element F6.2

Implement the audit plan

Performance criteria

You must ensure that

a) you allocate **audits** to competent people, taking account of their expertise, development needs and the need to provide equal opportunities

b) you provide sufficient support and advice to auditors to allow them to work effectively yet autonomously

c) you regularly monitor the progress of **audit** activity against the plan, and take appropriate **corrective action** in the event of significant variations

d) you provide **relevant people** with regular reports of progress against the plan.

Knowledge requirements

You need to know and understand

Communication
- the principles and processes of effective communication and how to apply them
- how to present progress reports

Equal opportunities
- the principles, organisational policies, values and legal requirements affecting equal opportunities at work.

Monitoring and evaluation
- how to monitor activities against plans, identify significant variations and decide on appropriate corrective action.

Organisational context
- the relevant structures, responsibilities and processes within the organisation
- the organisation's quality policy and procedures.

Quality management
- the principles of quality auditing and how to conduct an audit investigation
- the knowledge and skills required by those who will carry out the audits, and how to assess and develop these skills and knowledge.

Team working
- how to allocate work to a team based on their expertise, development needs and the need to provide equal opportunities for development to all competent people
- how to identify and provide the support and advice people need in order to work effectively yet autonomously.

Evidence requirements

You must prove that you *implement the audit plan* to the National Standard of competence.

To do this, you must provide evidence to convince your assessor that you consistently meet **all** the performance criteria.

Your evidence must be the result of real work activities undertaken by yourself. Evidence from simulated activities is acceptable **only** for performance criterion c) in this element.

You must show evidence that you implement **one** of the following types of **audits**
- within your organisation
- in other organisations.

You must also show evidence that you take **one** of the following types of **corrective action**
- changing audit activities
- changing the way resources are used for audit activities
- renegotiating the programme of audits.

You must also show evidence that you provide regular progress reports to **one** of the following types of **relevant people**
- higher-level managers or sponsors
- colleagues working at the same level as yourself
- quality specialists.

You must, however, convince your assessor that you have the necessary knowledge, understanding and skills to be able to perform competently in respect of **all** types of **audits**, **corrective action** and **relevant people**, listed above.

Monitor compliance with quality systems

Element F6.3

Report on compliance with quality systems

Performance criteria

You must ensure that

a) you accurately evaluate the results of quality **audits** against the organisation's quality objectives, relevant standards, legal requirements and industry best practice

b) you fully assess the appropriateness of the corrective action agreed to deal with discrepancies found during **audits**

c) you advise **relevant people**, with the appropriate level of urgency, of the risks associated with non-compliance discovered during **audits**

d) you report the findings of your evaluation to **relevant people** in accordance with organisational requirements

e) you give feedback to those whose performance was audited in a way which enhances their confidence and commitment to quality

f) you accurately assess your auditors' performance and implement appropriate development activities.

Knowledge requirements

You need to know and understand

Communication

- the principles and processes of effective communication and how to apply them
- how to report your findings
- how to give feedback in a way which enhances confidence and commitment.

Monitoring and evaluation

- how to evaluate the results of quality audits against the organisation's quality objectives, relevant standards, statutory requirements and industry best practice
- how to assess the appropriateness of corrective actions agreed.

Organisational context

- the relevant structures, responsibilities and processes within the organisation
- the organisation's quality objectives, policy and procedures
- the organisation's requirements for reporting on compliance with quality systems.

Quality management

- the principles of quality auditing and how to conduct an audit investigation
- how to assess the performance of auditors
- the knowledge and skills required by those who will carry out the audits, and how to assess and develop these skills and knowledge.

Evidence requirements

You must prove that you *report on compliance with quality systems* to the National Standard of competence.

To do this, you must provide evidence to convince your assessor that you consistently meet **all** the performance criteria.

Your evidence must be the result of real work activities undertaken by yourself. Evidence from simulated activities is **not** acceptable for this element.

You must show evidence that you evaluate the results of **one** of the following types of **audits**

- within your organisation
- in other organisations.

You must also show evidence that you report the findings of your evaluation to **one** of the following types of **relevant people**

- higher-level managers or sponsors
- colleagues working at the same level as yourself
- quality specialists.

You must, however, convince your assessor that you have the necessary knowledge, understanding and skills to be able to perform competently in respect of **all** types of **audits** and **relevant people**, listed above.

Carry out quality audits

Unit summary

This unit is about assessing the extent to which individuals and teams either within your organisation or in other organisations comply with agreed quality systems and procedures. It covers carrying out audits and reporting the results.

This unit contains two elements

F7.1 *Audit compliance with quality systems*
F7.2 *Follow up quality audits.*

Personal competencies

In performing effectively in this unit, you will show that you

Communicating
- adopt communication styles appropriate to listeners and situations, including selecting an appropriate time and place
- confirm listeners' understanding through questioning and interpretation of non-verbal signals
- encourage listeners to ask questions or rephrase statements to clarify their understanding

Influencing others
- present yourself positively to others

Searching for information
- seek information from multiple sources
- challenge the validity and reliability of sources of information
- push for concrete information in an ambiguous situation

Thinking and making decisions
- break processes down into tasks and activities
- identify a range of elements in and perspectives on a situation
- identify implications, consequences or causal relationships in a situation
- use your own experience and evidence from others to identify problems and understand situations
- take decisions which are realistic for the situation.

Carry out quality audits

Element F7.1

Audit compliance with quality systems

Performance criteria

You must ensure that

a) you carry out quality audits according to an agreed plan and schedule

b) you give **auditees** the required period of notice of your intention to audit

c) you clearly confirm the responsibilities of **auditees** and the procedures which apply to their work

d) your audit investigation is sufficiently detailed to reveal any discrepancies

e) for each discrepancy found, you agree with **auditees** appropriate corrective action and the date by which it should be carried out

f) you seek advice from **relevant people** if you cannot agree a discrepancy or corrective action with **auditees**

g) you conduct audits in a way which enhances the confidence and commitment to quality of **auditees**

h) you complete records of the quality audit in accordance with agreed procedures.

Knowledge requirements

You need to know and understand

Analytical techniques
- how to evaluate actual practice against procedures in order to identify discrepancies.

Communication
- the principles and processes of effective communication and how to apply them.

Information handling
- methods of seeking out information and how to apply them.

Involvement and motivation
- how to enhance the confidence and commitment of those being audited.

Organisational context
- the organisation's quality policies and procedures
- the organisation's plan and schedule for carrying out quality audits
- the organisation's structure and the responsibilities of people within it
- the people to turn to for advice on quality auditing issues
- the records of the quality audit that are required.

Quality management
- the period of notice of intention to audit required
- the procedures which apply to different people
- the principles of quality auditing and how to conduct an audit investigation
- how to identify appropriate corrective action and agree a reasonable date for it to be carried out.

Evidence requirements

You must prove that you *audit compliance with quality systems* to the National Standard of competence.

To do this, you must provide evidence to convince your assessor that you consistently meet **all** the performance criteria.

Your evidence must be the result of real work activities undertaken by yourself. Evidence from simulated activities is acceptable **only** for performance criterion f) in this element.

You must show evidence that you audit **one** of the following types of **auditees**
- individuals and teams within your organisation
- individuals and teams in other organisations.

You must also show evidence that you seek advice from **one** of the following types of **relevant people**
- higher-level managers or sponsors
- colleagues working at the same level as yourself
- quality specialists.

You must, however, convince your assessor that you have the necessary knowledge, understanding and skills to be able to perform competently in respect of **all** types of **auditees** and **relevant people**, listed above.

Carry out quality audits

Element F7.2

Follow up quality audits

Performance criteria

You must ensure that

a) you make your quality audit reports available to authorised people in accordance with the organisation's procedures

b) you promptly bring to the attention of **relevant people** any discrepancies which hold serious or immediate risks for the organisation

c) you check with **auditees** that corrective action has been carried out by the agreed dates

d) you report persistent problems in achieving compliance with quality systems to **relevant people**

e) you make appropriate recommendations for improvements to procedures to **relevant people**.

Knowledge requirements

You need to know and understand

Communication
- the principles and processes of effective communication and how to apply them
- how to make recommendations for improvements.

Organisational context
- the organisation's quality policies and procedures
- the organisation's plan and schedule for carrying out quality audits
- the organisation's structure and the responsibilities of people within it
- the people who are authorised to see quality audit reports.

Quality management
- the principles of quality auditing and how to conduct an audit investigation
- how to evaluate the risks which discrepancies may hold for the organisation
- the corrective action and dates agreed with auditees
- reports from auditors and how to interpret them.

Evidence requirements

You must prove that you *follow up quality audits* to the National Standard of competence.

To do this, you must provide evidence to convince your assessor that you consistently meet **all** the performance criteria.

Your evidence must be the result of real work activities undertaken by yourself. Evidence from simulated activities is acceptable **only** for performance criterion d) in this element.

You must show evidence that you make recommendations for improvements to **one** of the following types of **relevant people**
- higher-level managers or sponsors
- colleagues working at the same level as yourself
- quality specialists.

You must also show evidence that you check that corrective action has been carried out by **one** of the following types of **auditees**
- individuals and teams within your organisation
- individuals and teams in other organisations.

You must, however, convince your assessor that you have the necessary knowledge, understanding and skills to be able to perform competently in respect of **all** types of **relevant people** and **auditees**, listed above.

Contribute to project planning and preparation

Unit summary

This unit is about helping higher-level managers to plan and set up standard and complex projects which have operational or strategic implications for the project's sponsor. The sponsor may be internal or external to your organisation.

This unit contains three elements

G1.1 *Clarify the project's scope and definition*
G1.2 *Provide plans to achieve the project's goals*
G1.3 *Contribute to project preparation.*

Personal competencies

In performing effectively in this unit, you will show that you

Acting strategically
- display an understanding of how the different parts of the organisation and its environment fit together
- work towards a clearly defined vision of the future
- clearly relate your goals and actions to the strategic aims of the organisation
- take opportunities when they arise to achieve the longer-term aims or needs of the organisation

Communicating
- listen actively, ask questions, clarify points and rephrase others' statements to check mutual understanding

Focusing on results
- maintain a focus on objectives
- tackle problems and take advantage of opportunities as they arise
- prioritise objectives and schedule work to make the best use of time and resources

Influencing others
- develop and use contacts to trade information, and obtain support and resources
- present yourself positively to others
- create and prepare strategies for influencing others
- use a variety of means to influence others

Thinking and taking decisions
- produce a variety of solutions before taking a decision
- reconcile and make use of a variety of perspectives when making sense of a situation
- produce your own ideas from experience and practice
- take decisions which are realistic for the situation.

Contribute to project planning
and preparation

Element G1.1

Clarify the project's scope and definition

Performance criteria

You must ensure that

a) you identify with **relevant people**, the **project's** scope and definition to the level of detail needed for effective planning

b) you identify the links between the **project's** scope and definition and wider organisational objectives

c) you identify key **stakeholders'** interests in the **project**

d) you identify the main contingencies which may occur during the running of the **project**

e) you identify the main risks associated with the **project**

f) you provide realistic and informed views on the feasibility of the **project's** scope and definition to **relevant people**

g) you clearly establish your own level of responsibility and accountability for **project** activities, resources and decisions

h) you clearly confirm your understanding of the **project's** scope and definition with **relevant people** and take account of their feedback.

Knowledge requirements

You need to know and understand

Analytical techniques
- risk identification and assessment in project planning

Organisational context
- how projects interlink with and support wider organisational objectives and the importance of being aware of such links

Planning
- the importance of systematic and thorough planning to the success of projects
- the level of detail needed to start systematic project planning
- what constraints usually exist in projects (for example, time, resources, technology and legislation) and how to look for and identify the significance of constraints
- the importance of making an initial assessment of the feasibility of projects and how to do so
- contingency planning

Working relationships
- the importance of clarifying and agreeing the project's scope and definition and how to do this with relevant people
- the importance of maintaining effective working relationships with relevant people involved in the project and how to do so
- the importance of establishing your own level of responsibility in the project
- the importance of checking your understanding of the project with relevant people and taking account of their feedback.

Evidence requirements

You must prove that you *clarify the project's scope and definition* to the National Standard of competence.

To do this, you must provide evidence to convince your assessor that you consistently meet **all** the performance criteria.

Your evidence must be the result of real work activities undertaken by yourself. Evidence from simulated activities is **not** acceptable for this element.

You must show evidence that you confirm the project's scope and definition with at least **two** of the following types of **relevant people**
- higher-level managers
- colleagues
- specialists
- members of the sponsor's team.

You must show evidence that you clarify the scope and definition for at least **two** of the following types of **projects**
- with strategic implications for the sponsor
- with operational implications for the sponsor
- with a standard level of complexity
- with a high level of complexity

You must also show evidence that you identify **both** of the following types of **stakeholders** and their interests
- internal
- external.

You must, however, convince your assessor that you have the necessary knowledge, understanding and skills to be able to perform competently in respect of **all** types of **projects** and **relevant people** listed above.

Contribute to project planning
and preparation

Element G1.2

Provide plans to achieve the project's goals

Performance criteria

You must ensure that

a) your plans for the **project** are consistent with the agreed scope and definition and known **constraints**

b) you break the **project** work down into tasks which are manageable, measurable, and achievable

c) you specify links, dependencies, schedules, evaluation methods and handover procedures which are appropriate to the **project** and its work

d) you propose effective measures to deal with identified contingencies and risks

e) you realistically estimate and cost the human and physical resources required to carry out the **project's** tasks

f) you base your plans on previous experience and the good practice of **relevant people**

g) you check all aspects of the **project** plans with the **relevant people** and take account of their feedback when you make revisions.

Knowledge requirements

You need to know and understand

Planning

- the principles underpinning effective project planning
- different models of project planning and management
- how to break the work down into manageable, achievable and measurable tasks
- how to estimate the human and physical resources needed for projects
- the importance of specifying schedule, links, dependencies, monitoring and evaluation methods and handover and how to do so
- the importance of contingency and risk planning and how to do so
- the importance of using your own past experience and that of others and how to research and identify good practice

Working relationships

- the skills required to negotiate with relevant people involved in the project
- the importance of checking your plans with relevant people and taking account of their feedback, and how to do this.

Evidence requirements

You must prove that you *provide plans to achieve the project's goals* to the National Standard of competence.

To do this, you must provide evidence to convince your assessor that you consistently meet **all** the performance criteria.

Your evidence must be the result of real work activities undertaken by yourself. Evidence from simulated activities is **not** acceptable for this element.

You must show evidence that you provide plans for at least **two** of the following types of **projects**

- with strategic implications for the sponsor
- with operational implications for the sponsor
- with a standard level of complexity
- with a high level of complexity.

You must show evidence that your plans take account of at least **two** of the following types of **constraints**

- time
- resources
- available techniques
- organisational policies
- statutory and regulatory requirements.

You must also show evidence that you involve at least **two** of the following types of **relevant people**

- higher-level managers
- colleagues
- members of the sponsor's team
- specialists.

You must, however, convince your assessor that you have the necessary knowledge, understanding and skills to be able to perform competently in respect of **all** types of **relevant people**, **projects** and **constraints** listed above.

Contribute to project planning
and preparation

Element G1.3

Contribute to project preparation

Performance criteria

You must ensure that

a) you assist in the selection of **team members** who are able to make an effective contribution to the **project's** objectives

b) you recommend roles for the **project** team, and allocate tasks in a way which is realistic and equitable

c) you recommend clear lines of responsibility and accountability which take account of **team members'** other responsibilities

d) you recommend meeting schedules, reporting, control and communication methods which are consistent with the **project** plans

e) you contribute to effective opportunities for team development

f) you research and recommend feasible and cost-effective methods of obtaining the necessary **physical resources**

g) you research and recommend efficient and effective methods of managing the necessary **physical resources** and finances which are consistent with organisational requirements

h) you check all aspects of the **project's** resourcing and control methods with **relevant people** and take account of their feedback when making revisions.

Knowledge requirements

You need to know and understand

Communication
- the importance of having good communications and how to maximise the effectiveness and efficiency of communications

Organisational context
- the organisational requirements which are relevant to managing resources and finance

Project management
- how to allocate project roles and tasks equitably and realistically
- the importance of having clear lines of responsibility and accountability within the project and how to establish these, especially where line management responsibility is shared
- the importance and purpose of control methods and how to select and propose methods appropriate to different types of projects

Recruitment and selection
- how to identify and specify the competences, skills and knowledge which project team members need
- how to obtain the people you require to staff projects, taking account of equality of opportunity

Resource management
- the importance of tight financial and resource controls, and what methods may be used

Training and development
- the importance of team development and the contributions you can make to this.

Evidence requirements

You must prove that you *contribute to project preparation* to the National Standard of competence.

To do this, you must provide evidence to convince your assessor that you consistently meet **all** the performance criteria.

Your evidence must be the result of real work activities undertaken by yourself. Evidence from simulated activities is **not** acceptable for this element.

You must show evidence that you help to select at least **one** of the following types of **team members**
- people exclusively involved in the project
- people who have other responsibilities and accountabilities

You must show evidence that you establish resourcing and control for at least **two** of the following types of **projects**
- with strategic implications for the sponsor
- with operational implications for the sponsor
- with a standard level of complexity
- with a high level of complexity.

You must show evidence that you deal with **one** of the following types of **physical resources**
- from within your organisation
- from outside your organisation.

You must also show evidence that you involve at least **two** of the following types of **relevant people**
- higher-level manager
- colleagues
- specialists

You must, however, convince your assessor that you have the necessary knowledge, understanding and skills to be able to perform competently in respect of **all** types of **team members**, **projects**, **physical resources** and **relevant people** listed above.

Co-ordinate the running of projects

Unit summary

This unit is about co-ordinating the work of standard and complex projects which have operational or strategic implications for the sponsor. The sponsor may be internal or external to your organisation.

This unit contains three elements

G2.1 *Support the project team*
G2.2 *Co-ordinate activities, resources and plans*
G2.3 *Keep stakeholders informed of project progress*.

Personal competencies

In performing effectively in this unit, you will show that you

Acting assertively

- take a leading role in initiating action and making decisions
- take personal responsibility for making things happen
- take control of situations and events
- act in an assured and unhesitating manner when faced with a challenge
- state your own position and views clearly in conflict situations

Communicating

- listen actively, ask questions, clarify points and rephrase others' statements to check mutual understanding
- identify the information needs of listeners
- adopt communication styles appropriate to listeners and situations, including selecting an appropriate time and place
- use a variety of media and communication aids to reinforce points and maintain interest
- present difficult ideas and problems in ways that promote understanding

Focusing on results

- maintain a focus on objectives
- tackle problems and take advantage of opportunities as they arise
- prioritise objectives and schedule work to make the best use of time and resources

Thinking and taking decisions

- produce a variety of solutions before taking a decision
- reconcile and make use of a variety of perspectives when making sense of a situation
- produce your own ideas from experience and practice
- take decisions which are realistic for the situation.

Co-ordinate the running of projects

Element G2.1

Support the project team

Performance criteria

You must ensure that

a) you consistently motivate **team members** to fulfil the tasks allocated to them with commitment and enthusiasm

b) you consistently provide **team members** with clear, accurate and up-to-date information appropriate to the role which they play in the **project**

c) you provide opportunities for **team members** to undertake activities which will contribute to their own development and that of the **project**

d) you actively seek information from **team members** on **project** progress and their views on the **project's** effectiveness

e) you identify problems which **team members** are experiencing in good time to take remedial action

f) you provide **team members** with the support and encouragement they need to achieve their objectives throughout the lifetime of the **project.**

Knowledge requirements

You need to know and understand

Involvement and motivation

- methods which may be used to motivate team members and gain their commitment
- the importance of keeping team members properly informed as to their roles in the project and effective methods to make this happen
- the importance of enabling team members to contribute to their own development and that of the project and different methods of achieving this

Leadership styles

- the principles which underpin the effective co-ordination of projects and your role in relation to this
- styles of leadership which are effective in managing projects

Providing support

- the importance of providing support to team members during projects
- the types of problems which team members and stakeholders may experience
- the types of support which team members may need during projects and how to identify and provide such support.

Evidence requirements

You must prove that you *support the project team* to the National Standard of competence.

To do this, you must provide evidence to convince your assessor that you consistently meet **all** the performance criteria.

Your evidence must be the result of real work activities undertaken by yourself. Evidence from simulated activities is **not** acceptable for this element.

You must show evidence that you work with at least **one** of the following types of **team members**

- people exclusively involved in the project
- people who have other responsibilities and accountabilities.

You must show evidence that you support teams in at least **two** of the following types of **projects**

- with strategic implications for the sponsor
- with operational implications for the sponsor
- with a standard level of complexity
- with a high level of complexity.

You must, however, convince your assessor that you have the necessary knowledge, understanding and skills to be able to perform competently in respect of **all** types of **team members** and **projects** listed above.

Co-ordinate the running of
projects

Element G2.2

Co-ordinate activities, resources and plans

Performance criteria

You must ensure that

a) you **monitor** and **evaluate project** work in a way which is consistent with the agreed plans

b) you accurately measure progress against plans and identify emerging risks and difficulties and their causes

c) you obtain clear authorisation for all stages of work to start, continue or finish

d) you clearly inform your higher-level manager of any emerging problems or risks in good time for remedial action to be taken

e) you keep activities and **resources** in line with the **project's** plans or seek approval from the higher-level manager for any amendments to plans and **resources**

f) you recommend changes in **project** activities, plans and **resources** in a way which keeps disruption to a minimum

g) you make any adjustments to activities, **resources** and plans with the knowledge and agreement of the team and accurately record and store these adjustments

h) you inform the higher-level manager promptly and clearly of any need to review the **project's** scope and definition with the sponsor.

Knowledge requirements

You need to know and understand

Analytical techniques
- how to identify and assess emerging risks

Change management
- the importance of managing change in projects and how to minimise disruption wherever possible

Project management
- awareness of different project management methods and their possible uses
- methods to monitor and evaluate project progress effectively
- the importance of obtaining authorisation for all stages of work to start, continue or finish according to your evaluation of progress
- why activities need to be kept in line with the plans for the project and control methods to ensure this

Resource management
- why resources need to be tightly controlled and methods to achieve this

Working relationships
- why higher-level managers need to be promptly and clearly informed of any implications for the project's scope and definition
- why you should have the agreement of team members in order to adjust activities, resources and plans
- who needs to be consulted on what kinds of changes
- how to negotiate adjustments to the satisfaction of all those involved.

Evidence requirements

You must prove that you *co-ordinate activities, resources and plans* to the National Standard of competence.

To do this, you must provide evidence to convince your assessor that you consistently meet **all** the performance criteria.

Your evidence must be the result of real work activities undertaken by yourself. Evidence from simulated activities is **only** acceptable for performance criterion h).

You must show evidence that you use **both** of the following types of **monitoring** and **evaluation**
- by direct observation of activities
- by considering reports from others.

You must show evidence that you co-ordinate **two** of the following types of **resources**
- physical resources
- people
- financial resources.

You must show evidence that you monitor and co-ordinate at least **two** of the following types of **projects**
- with strategic implications for the sponsor
- with operational implications for the sponsor
- with a standard level of complexity
- with a high level of complexity.

You must, however, convince your assessor that you have the necessary knowledge, understanding and skills to be able to perform competently in respect of **all** types of **resources** and **projects** listed above.

Co-ordinate the running of
projects

Element G2.3

Keep stakeholders informed of project progress

Performance criteria

You must ensure that

a) you provide the key **stakeholders** with timely, forward-looking and relevant information which is consistent with the **project** plans

b) you provide **team members** and higher-level managers with effective opportunities to contribute to the information you provide

c) the content of the information meets your **stakeholders'** needs, while maintaining agreements on confidentiality

d) you provide information in styles and formats most appropriate to the types of **stakeholders** involved

e) your distribution methods are effective in reaching the key **stakeholders**

f) you actively seek and assess information from **stakeholders** which may affect the running of the **project**.

Knowledge requirements

You need to know and understand

Communication

- the methods which may be used to keep stakeholders up-to-date and how to agree methods appropriate to different groups
- how to select content, styles, format and distribution methods for different audiences and the importance of doing so

Information handling

- the importance of ensuring information is consistent with agreements on confidentiality

Involvement and motivation

- the importance of involving other relevant people in producing information
- the contributions other relevant people can make to information and how to involve them

Organisational context

- the range of stakeholders you need to keep informed

Working relationships

- the importance of keeping all key stakeholders informed on project progress.

Evidence requirements

You must prove that you *keep stakeholders informed of project progress* to the National Standard of competence.

To do this, you must provide evidence to convince your assessor that you consistently meet **all** the performance criteria.

Your evidence must be the result of real work activities undertaken by yourself. Evidence from simulated activities is **not** acceptable for this element.

You must show evidence that you inform **one** of the following types of **stakeholders**
- internal
- external.

You must show evidence that you provide information for at least **two** of the following types of **projects**
- with strategic implications for the sponsor
- with operational implications for the sponsor
- with a standard level of complexity
- with a high level of complexity.

You must show evidence that you involve **one** of the following types of **team members**
- people exclusively involved in the project
- people who have other responsibilities and accountabilities.

You must, however, convince your assessor that you have the necessary knowledge, understanding and skills to be able to perform competently in respect of **all** types of **stakeholders**, **projects** and **team members** listed above.

Contribute to project closure

Unit summary

This unit is about helping to complete standard and complex projects which have operational or strategic implications for the sponsor. The sponsor may be internal or external to your organisation.

This unit contains two elements

G3.1 *Complete project activities*
G3.2 *Contribute to the evaluation of project planning and implementation.*

Personal competencies

In performing effectively in this unit, you will show that you

Acting assertively

- take a leading role in initiating action and making decisions
- take personal responsibility for making things happen
- take control of situations and events
- act in an assured and unhesitating manner when faced with a challenge
- say no to unreasonable requests
- state your own position and views clearly in conflict situations
- maintain your beliefs, commitment and effort in spite of set-backs or opposition

Communicating

- listen actively, ask questions, clarify points and rephrase others' statements to check mutual understanding
- adopt communication styles appropriate to listeners and situations, including selecting an appropriate time and place
- present difficult ideas and problems in ways that promote understanding

Focusing on results

- maintain a focus on objectives
- tackle problems and take advantage of opportunities as they arise
- focus personal attention on specific details that are critical to the success of a key event
- actively seek to do things better
- use change as an opportunity for improvement
- establish and communicate high expectations of performance, including setting an example to others
- monitor quality of work and progress against plans
- continually strive to identify and minimise barriers to excellence.

Contribute to project closure

Element G3.1

Complete project activities

Performance criteria

You must ensure that

a) you confirm that all the **project's** goals have been achieved to the agreed schedule, costs and quality criteria

b) all deliverables are handed over according to agreed procedures

c) you resolve any handover problems to the sponsor's satisfaction or seek the support of **relevant people**

d) you clearly inform your higher-level manager that the agreed **project** outcomes have been achieved and seek their approval to close the **project**

e) you collect information from **relevant people** on the effectiveness of the **project** and their level of satisfaction with it

f) you confirm the completion of the **project** with the team and promptly bring all associated work to an end in a way which is consistent with your **project** plans

g) you complete all the necessary procedures relating to finance, resources and personnel in accordance with organisational requirements

h) all records and documents relating to the **project** are accurate, complete and securely stored for future use.

Knowledge requirements

You need to know and understand

Customer relations
- common difficulties which may occur at the point of handover and how to address these
- how to maintain an effective working relationship with the sponsor at the point of project closure
- the importance of obtaining the sponsor's agreement that all specified work has been carried out

Monitoring and evaluation
- methods of ensuring that the agreed deliverables have been provided
- the importance of storing records and documents for future use

Organisational context
- procedures for finance, resources and personnel which need to be followed at project closure and why
- the records and documents which need to be completed and why

Planning
- the plans for project closure
- the handover procedures for the project.

Evidence requirements

You must prove that you *complete project activities* to the National Standard of competence.

To do this, you must provide evidence to convince your assessor that you consistently meet **all** the performance criteria.

Your evidence must be the result of real work activities undertaken by yourself. Evidence from simulated activities is **only** acceptable for performance criterion c).

You must show evidence that you complete the work of at least **two** of the following types of **projects**
- with strategic implications for the sponsor
- with operational implications for the sponsor
- with a standard level of complexity
- with a high level of complexity.

You must also show evidence that you involve at least **two** of the following types of **relevant people**
- higher-level manager
- team members
- colleagues
- specialists.

You must, however, convince your assessor that you have the necessary knowledge, understanding and skills to be able to perform competently in respect of **all** types of **projects** and **relevant people** listed above.

Contribute to project closure

Element G3.2

Contribute to the evaluation of project planning and implementation

Performance criteria

You must ensure that

a) you collect, check and collate information relating to the planning and implementation of the **project** in a way which will assist effective **evaluation**

b) you include information which covers the perspectives of all key stakeholders

c) you assist **relevant people** to compare what was planned, what actually happened and what changes had to be made to plans, **project** scope and definition

d) you propose feasible causes for variations to plans and the key lessons to be drawn from the **project**

e) you record and store your **evaluation** in a way which can be used to inform future **projects**.

Knowledge requirements

You need to know and understand

Involvement and motivation

- the importance of involving other relevant people in the evaluation and methods to ensure their contributions are effective

Monitoring and evaluation

- the principles underpinning the monitoring and evaluation of projects and your role in relation to this
- how to identify, collect, verify and collate key information which will assist the evaluation
- how to identify the reasons for changes in project plans and implementation

Training and development

- how to identify the key lessons from an evaluation and why it is important to record and store evaluation results for future use.

Evidence requirements

You must prove that you *contribute to the evaluation of project planning and implementation* to the National Standard of competence.

To do this, you must provide evidence to convince your assessor that you consistently meet **all** the performance criteria.

Your evidence must be the result of real work activities undertaken by yourself. Evidence from simulated activities is **not** acceptable for this element.

You must show evidence that you evaluate at least **two** of the following types of **projects**

- with strategic implications for the sponsor
- with operational implications for the sponsor
- with a standard level of complexity
- with a high level of complexity.

You must show evidence that you use **both** of the following types of **evaluation**

- quantitative
- qualitative.

You must also show evidence that you involve **two** of the following types of **relevant people**

- higher-level manager
- colleagues
- team members
- members of the sponsor's team.

You must, however, convince your assessor that you have the necessary knowledge, understanding and skills to be able to perform competently in respect of **all** types of **projects** and **relevant people** listed above.

Index

Notes
1. Page references for major topics of units are in **bold**
2. The sub-entry *teams* should be taken throughout to indicate *teams and individuals*